ALL SORTS OF
SORTS

Word Sorts for Complex Spelling and Phonetic Pattern Reinforcement

by Sheron Brown

A Teaching Resource Center Publication

Published by
Teaching Resource Center
P.O. Box 82777, San Diego, CA 92138
1-800-833-3389
www.trcabc.com

Edited by Laura Woodard
Design & production by Janis Poe

PRINTED IN THE UNITED STATES OF AMERICA ISBN:1-56785-053-7

Table of Contents

CVC, CVCC, CVVC, and VCCV Syllable Structures

Stressed First and Second Syllable Words

Abstract Vowel Sounds of "A"

Adding Plural Endings

Open and Closed Syllable Structures With Short and Long Vowel Sounds

Long Vowel Patterns in the Stressed Syllable

Short and Long Vowel Patterns in the Stressed Syllable

R-Controlled Vowel Patterns in the Stressed Syllable

Abstract Vowel Combinations in the Stressed Syllable

Abstract Vowel Combinations in the Unstressed Syllable

Common Prefixes

Common Suffixes

Final "K" Variations

Consonant Alternations With Suffixes "ion" and "sion"

Adding the Suffixes "able" and "ible" to Base and Root Words

Adding "ing" to Multisyllabic Words

Forming More Complex Plural Endings

Common Prefixes: anti, auto, cat, circum

Common Prefixes: inter, intra, mal, peri

Common Prefixes: post, pro, super, trans

Number-Related Prefixes

Common Greek Root Words

Common Latin Root Words

Appendix

Introduction

A Guide for Using Word Sorts in the Classroom

Students acquire their knowledge of words, sounds, patterns and meaning relationships in a variety of ways, but word acquisition itself follows a very predictable developmental path. At the earliest developmental stage in word study, the *letter name* stage, the student learns beginning and ending letters and then begins to recognize short and then long vowels in the middle of the words they are learning to read and write. As a student's bank of known words and word patterns begins to grow, he or she moves to the next developmental stage, the *within word* stage, and begins to concentrate on the common vowel patterns and the vowel combinations found within words. Students also explore and learn consonant blends, vowel digraphs, and common endings at this stage. The next developmental stage, the *syllable juncture* stage, focuses on syllables, including stressed and unstressed syllables, closed and open syllables, and the very common prefixes and suffixes that are added to the base and root words being studied. At the last stage of word study, the *derivational constancy* stage, students are on their way to a thorough understanding of how words are formed and what their meanings are, which includes learning the many Latin and Greek root words that so many English words are derived from. At this advanced developmental stage, students explore more prefixes and suffixes and the spelling, pronunciation, and meaning changes made when adding these affixes to roots to form word derivatives. The word sorts in this book have been designed for students in last three stages of development.

The decision about where to focus the student's word work depends on two things: teacher observation and student assessment results. By observing the types of spelling errors found in each student's writing, and by administering a spelling inventory assessment such as those described in *Word Journeys* by Kathy Ganske and *Words Their Way* by Donald R. Bear, Marcia Invernizzi, Shane Templeton and Francine

Johnston, a teacher can quickly identify each student's stage of development in spelling. The teacher can then determine which word sorts in this book are most appropriate for each student's word study activities. The students may then be placed into small groups for word study work, including word sorting, based on their stage of development in spelling.

Using the sorts in this book, your students will acquire word pattern knowledge, learn spelling rules, and formulate generalizations through compare-and-contrast activities. They'll learn to sort groups of words according to spelling rules, meanings, endings, sound patterns, prefixes, suffixes, spelling generalizations, syllables, and other shared properties.

The various word sorts may be used as individual, small group, or whole class activities. All you need to make it happen is this book, a copy machine, a baggie or envelope for word card storage, and scissors! Each sort is designed to be used as an open, closed, speed, blind, or writing sort, depending on the teacher's lesson objective that day. These five different kinds of word sorts are explained in detail on page VII of the introduction.

There are almost as many types of word sorts as there are words and subject areas. As students' knowledge of words and word patterns increases, the sorting possibilities across all curricular areas increase as well. Students may begin to sort by prefixes, suffixes, vowel phonograms, roots, accented and unaccented syllables, and word meanings and move into more complex sorts as their word knowledge grows. Any skills or concepts you are teaching your students in any curricular area can conceivably be turned into a word sort! Blank word sort blacklines have been included in the appendix to enable you to design your own sorts to further meet your students' word study and vocabulary needs across the curriculum.

Why do word sorts?

- Word sorts enable students to attend to the structure of words in print as they carefully examine the letters and patterns in each word to determine how to categorize it.
- Students learn classification skills as they discover how sets of words they are given might be alike.
- Word sorts allow a teacher to assess each student's understanding of the many phonetic, spelling, and word identification strategies being taught in the classroom.
- Word sorts are easy-to-check assessment tools that enable a teacher to quickly evaluate a student's understanding of a strategy without resorting to the usual paper and pencil test format.
- Word sorts provide a multi-sensory experience as students read, sort, manipulate, and categorize words in multiple ways.
- Word sorts allow students to look at words from their various levels of knowledge about how words work.
- Students are able to apply their word knowledge in an organized, yet pleasing and fun format.
- Students are empowered to make their own decisions about word categories based on their personal knowledge of words.

Glossary of Word Sort Terms

The different types of word sorts explained below represent various levels of difficulty and should be presented to students in the following order:

1. **open sort** – The teacher provides only the words, and the students decide the sort categories based on what they see. Open sorts are valuable, as they provide a window for the teacher into each student's word work and which features they are noticing or not noticing.

2. **closed sort** – The teacher provides the categories for the word sort. Closed sorts are used more frequently than open sorts, as they allow the teacher to focus students' attention on a word feature, characteristic, or pattern the class is currently studying. Closed sorts are also valuable assessment tools. The teacher can rapidly assess student understanding of word features by simply checking the students' sorts against the Answer Keys (pages 176-209).

3. **speed sort** – This is usually a timed sort that students can do once they are adept at sorting words. Speed sorts are excellent for building fluency and accuracy when working with known patterns and concepts. Students can record the time it takes to sort a given set of words and then try to beat their records.

4. **blind sort** – This is a closed sort in which the teacher calls out the words and the students point to or say the categories they see listed on the worksheet or written on the board or overhead. Blind sorts are particularly useful when the teacher wants to focus on the sound patterns rather than the visual patterns of the words.

5. **writing sort** – The students have key words, provided by the teacher, written as column headers. They write words under the appropriate categories as the teacher calls them out, using the key words as spelling guides. Writing sorts focus on both auditory and visual patterns in words and are a combination of closed and blind sorts.

Modeling the Word Sorts
An Instructional Format

After assessing your students' skills and determining their word development stage, select a word sort that you will be assigning an individual, a small group, or the whole class based on their assessment results. Instruct your students to set aside any words they cannot read. Students can only be expected to sort words that they know or can read independently. When selecting appropriate word sorts for your students, make sure you have taught the word features, rules, generalizations, or concepts of the sort so the students can truly benefit from the compare-and-contrast activity that sorting involves.

Introduce the concept of word sorting with an *open sort* first. Make copies of the selected word sort, but **do not give the students the category cards at the top.** Since an open sort means that the students determine the word sort categories based on similarities and differences *they* notice in the words, the students should not see the category cards until they are finished with the open sort. Instruct the students to cut apart the word cards and organize them according to whatever categories or patterns they "see." When all students have finished their word sorts, have volunteers share how they chose to organize the word cards. List the categories on the board or overhead projector so that all students can see the many different ways their classmates have chosen to organize the word cards. **Be accepting of all word categories students share** as long as they can explain how they organized their cards. After all, an "open sort" means that category choices are truly "open."

After your students are comfortable with an open sort, introduce them to a *closed sort*. Copy the selected blackline master for the sort, and have the students place the category cards at the top of their desks or tables. Show the students how to look carefully at each word card to determine the correct category for it. Model the process of checking the words under each category card to ensure that all of the words placed there share the common characteristic of that category. If the selected blackline contains an **OUT OF SORTS** category card,

demonstrate how certain words will not fit into any of the other categories and therefore belong under the **OUT OF SORTS** category card.

After students have completed the closed sort and are comfortable with the closed sort process, introduce them to the *speed sort*. Do not have your students do a speed sort unless they have already done a closed sort with the word cards, since a speed sort depends on your students' familiarity with the words being sorted. Instruct your students to leave the category cards at the top of their desks or tables and have them turn the word cards facedown and mix them up. At your signal the students are to turn them over and place them under the correct category cards as quickly as they can. Instruct them to raise their hands when they have completed the sort and have checked their cards. Record the time it took the first student to correctly sort the cards, and challenge the students to "beat" the posted time by doing the sort again. This is a fun way to have your students read and reread the word sort cards as they quickly sort them into the given categories. A variation of the speed sort is to make a transparency of the word sort, cut it apart, and set the timer. Talk aloud about the words and what you are noticing as you sort them into the correct categories on the overhead. After you have completed the sort, model checking it and then post your time on the board. Then, challenge your students to beat your time. You will find that your students will gladly sort and re-sort their words in an attempt to have the fastest sort time. Speed sorts are a wonderful way to provide multiple opportunities for your students to learn word patterns.

Teaching your students to do a *blind sort* will help them sharpen their auditory discrimination skills, because they do not see the word sort cards, but focus instead on the auditory patterns in the words. Students place the category cards on their desks, leaving the word sort cards in their storage baggies or envelopes. The teacher calls out one of the word sort words and the students can point to, call out, or pick up and show the correct cate-

continued on next page

gory card for that word. The teacher may call out some or all of the words in the sort. Blind sorts are particularly useful when you want to focus on the sound patterns, rather than the visual patterns, in a set of words.

A *writing sort* will help your students focus on both auditory and visual patterns in words. Have them write the categories of the sort at the top of a blank lined paper or on blank category cards (see Appendix, page 172), leaving enough room to

write dictated words in columns under each category. Also have them write one example word under each category heading to serve as a spelling guide. After all of the words have been dictated and written by the students on their lined paper or on the blank word sort cards, share the word sort answers. The correct word sort may be shown on the board or overhead in order for students to correct their spelling and sorting of the dictated words.

Using the Word Sorts in this Book

- For an *open sort*, copy only the words below the dotted line, and let the students use the extra strips of paper from the sides to create their own category cards.

- For a *closed sort*, make copies of the entire word sort blackline for the students. Have them cut apart the words and sort them into the categories provided.

- Another technique for sorting with the class is to make a transparency of the sort for the overhead. Have the students copy the words onto the blank word sort blackline (pages 172-173) and then cut them apart and sort them. Or you can have them copy the words from the overhead onto lined paper they have folded into columns, or into a word study notebook.

- Students may work with partners to sort the word cards into the appropriate categories. They may then write them on a separate piece of paper or copy them into a word study notebook for reinforcement.

- You can laminate and cut apart the word sort blacklines and store them in envelopes in a *word sort learning center.* See pages 174-175 for Center Cards. You may want to keep the Answer Keys (pages 176-209) in a file in the learning center so students can either check their com-

pleted word sorts themselves or have a "designated checker" do it for them.

- The word sort format is an excellent assessment tool to ensure that the word sounds, patterns, spelling rules and concepts you have taught have indeed been learned. Use the results to quickly identify students who need additional instruction and practice with the word sort concepts before attempting the sort again.

- You may have students revisit certain word sorts on another day by having them not only re-sort the words, but also put them in alphabetical order once they are in the correct categories. This helps build sight recognition of the words as well as practicing alphabetization skills.

- Students should keep the cut-up word sort words in an envelope or a plastic baggie so they are handy for the various additional activities suggested in this book.

- Students should also have a separate section in their three-ring binders for word study activities, or have a composition book with lined paper where they keep their word sort written activities.

- After your students have been taught the spelling concepts and/or word patterns, they can be assigned any of the word study activities detailed below.

continued on next page

- You can introduce a new word sort by playing the **"Guess My Sorts" game.** Pass out the selected word sort (**without the category markers**) and have each student or small group of students place a paper numbered from 1 to 5 at their work center. Have the students cut out the words and sort them into categories as they "see" them, without using category headings. Then, give the students a short period of time, perhaps three to five minutes, to visit five other work centers. You may wish to select just one or two students from each group for this. They are to study the sort of the person or group they are visiting, and then write their name by one line on the numbered sheet, followed by the categories they think the words were sorted into. If a student visits a work center where all five lines on the numbered paper have been filled in, they must move on to another work center. After time is up, individual students or groups may share how they sorted their words and how many people guessed correctly. You can then pass out the category cards and have the students sort the words into those categories.

- Gather three students who are all working on the same word sort. Provide one student with the sort answer key (see Appendix, pages 176-209) and a digital timer. This student will be the "checker." Have the other two students put the category cards at the top of their work surfaces and turn the word sort cards facedown. When the checker starts the timer and says, "Begin," the other two students are to sort their word cards. The first student to complete the word sort raises a hand, and the other "sorter" must stop working. The checker stops the timer and uses the answer key to check the completed sort. If it's correct, the "winning" student becomes the checker and the other two students sort the word cards while the checker keeps time. If incorrect, the timer is restarted and the process begins again. This format provides multiple opportunities for students to practice the word sort patterns in a small group setting as they take the roles of "checker" and "sorters."

- Using an open-ended game board and one set of sort cards, play a word sorting board game with two to three students. Put the category cards out and the word sort cards facedown. One student acts as "checker" and has the sort answer key. The players each pick a colored game marker. Each player, in turn, rolls one die, selects a word sort card, reads the word, and places the sort card under the correct category card. If the checker says the player sorted the word correctly, the player may move his or her marker the number of spaces rolled on the die. The game continues until one player wins. The game may be replayed numerous times with different students taking the role of "checker."

- Two students who are doing the same word sort can work as partners, taking turns doing the sort individually. One student sorts, and the other checks using the sort answer key. Then the roles reverse.

- After students have had multiple opportunities to interact with a particular word sort, they may copy the completed sort into their word study books along with a "generalization" about why the words were sorted the way they were. They should title the word sort (using the category cards) and add the title and page number to their book's table of contents.

- After students have had some practice with a word sort, send them on a hunt for additional words that fit into the sort categories. They may use any printed texts found in the room, including dictionaries. The additional words may be shared with the class or within small groups. The students may also add the words to their word study books. They should mark these additional words with a check mark or star to distinguish them from the words found in the original word sort.

- As a final activity, the students may be directed to arrange the word sort and category cards on a sheet of legal-sized paper and glue them in place. This is an excellent homework or learning center activity.

short a	short e	short i
short o	short u	

---

sack	rap	lead
tick	plum	hymn
cell	it's	nit
him	tic	wrap
knot	plumb	read
in	sell	red
its	tacks	tax
knit	bread	cent
sent	inn	not
led	bred	sac

short a	short e	OUT OF SORTS
short i	short o	short u

cent	peak	rap
led	plum	bread
knot	inn	cell
in	sell	its
wrap	plumb	bred
tic	sent	knit
sac	lead	it's
tick	bare	tacks
peek	sack	nit
tax	not	bear

long a	long e	long i
long o	long u	

maid	blew	deer
I	chute	high
hole	die	weed
hi	peace	role
we'd	main	meet
steal	eye	Maine
oh	made	dye
meat	whole	shoot
dear	steel	blue
roll	owe	piece

long a	long e	OUT OF SORTS
long i	long o	long u

feet	flu	grown
in	close	sight
creek	I'll	write
groan	vain	know
site	sell	dough
right	no	pale
cell	feat	week
doe	inn	flue
pail	vane	clothes
weak	creak	aisle

short vowel homophones	long vowel homophones

- -

bin	you	tale
hay	tax	stake
which	cheap	inn
loan	beet	cent
rose	bail	reel
real	rows	beat
tail	lone	bale
steak	been	ewe
in	witch	tacks
sent	hey	cheep

short vowel homophones	long vowel homophones	OUT OF SORTS

witch	knot	flee
so	earn	plain
sun	seam	knead
fowl	sent	stile
flea	hymn	urn
plane	foul	weigh
need	him	rap
style	which	not
way	sew	seem
wrap	son	cent

homophones

not homophones

way-weigh	say-stay	deer-dear
male-mail	pear-pair	house-home
farm-harm	their-there	peace-piece
plain-plane	hey-hay	break-brake
name-names	might-light	can-cannot
rain-rein	cell-sell	wave-waved
tale-tail	beech-beach	passed-past
shame-blame	tax-tacks	steak-stake
prays-praise	cake-cakes	run-running
air-heir	base-bass	red-read

homophones
not homophones

peak-peek	be-see	they're-there
sleigh-slay	ant-aunt	ate-eight
hair-hare	cash-cache	bale-bail
sled-sleigh	seem-seam	see-saw
need-knead	set-seat	jeans-genes
pale-pail	most-boast	don't-did not
need-needs	fair-fare	meet-meat
main-mane	praise-preys	bear-bare
rap-wrap	rain-reign	was-were
sail-sale	can't-cannot	ran-fan

compounds

not compounds

- -

farmhouse	windstorm	cushion
outline	isn't	typewriter
update	landslide	thanksgiving
coming	sugar	flashlight
eyelid	notebook	handmade
nightmare	monster	magazine
headlight	snowy	throughout
table	snowstorm	monkey
dispenser	toothache	skyscraper
pitcher	upset	horse

compounds

not compounds

pancakes	waffle	dictionary
waterproof	cornhusk	courthouse
everybody	telephone	rainy
overflow	hairstyle	grounded
picture	senator	basketball
coastline	bridge	upright
counter	lighter	cornstarch
coffee	headlight	mountainous
puppies	footbridge	plowed
newsstand	windshield	toothpaste

two-syllable compounds	three-syllable compounds

- -

outside	underground	typewriter
horseshoe	hillside	footbridge
afternoon	network	barefoot
seasick	waterproof	downstream
summertime	overboard	understand
thanksgiving	policeman	businessman
paintbrush	chairman	flowerpot
cheerleader	butterscotch	withdraw
broadcast	grandfather	sailboat
anywhere	scarecrow	stagecoach

two-syllable compounds	three-syllable compounds

- -

proofread	waterproof	weekend
smallpox	grandson	grandchildren
townspeople	withhold	candlestick
hillside	coffeepot	drugstore
salesperson	teapot	however
mountainside	forever	buttermilk
anything	paintbrush	spaceship
steamboat	rowboat	quarterback
starfish	everyone	otherwise
undermine	underline	within

two-syllable compounds	three-syllable compounds	

---

sailboat	pitcher	basketball
afternoon	broomstick	football
grandmother	hillside	toothpaste
shepherd	pencil	peppermill
within	notebook	soapbox
underground	summertime	shoeshine
masterpiece	cornstarch	headlight
everyone	slowly	stagecoach
however	anywhere	snowstorm
tablecloth	pancakes	raindrops

two-syllable compounds	three-syllable compounds

withhold	offspring	whenever
pancake	grandchildren	anytime
overall	waterfall	masterpiece
forever	flashlight	mainland
network	buttermilk	flagpole
typewriter	without	skyscraper
rooftop	starfish	summertime
scarecrow	wildlife	understand
underline	highway	grandfather
everyone	football	thanksgiving

two-syllable compounds	three-syllable compounds

- -

highway	butterscotch	basketball
indoor	waterproof	baseball
everyone	without	rattlesnake
gingerbread	stagecoach	policeman
snowflake	fireplace	fireman
overall	textbook	windowpane
warehouse	birthday	astronaut
flashlight	outside	afternoon
anything	headlight	however
paintbrush	hamburger	bedroom

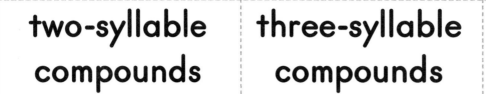

two-syllable compounds	three-syllable compounds	OUT OF SORTS

- -

peanut	salesperson	satisfaction
summertime	proofread	typewriter
playing	goldfish	starfish
whoever	propeller	everyone
rattlesnake	storekeeper	quarterback
refrigerator	overcast	steamboat
weekend	warehouse	smallpox
overlook	wildlife	waterway
flowerpot	mountainside	fingerprint
without	worthwhile	flashlight

contractions

not contractions

who's	they'll	that's
where	how's	can't
you'd	we'd	they're
isn't	you're	what
he'll	here	cannot
she	here's	should
doesn't	would	don't
his	shouldn't	had
I've	that	into
they	what's	aren't

contractions

not contractions

wouldn't	hers	would've
was	don't	haven't
within	there's	you're
hasn't	who'd	they're
you've	yours	went
hadn't	that	that'll
he'll	does	your
theirs	aren't	doesn't
who's	how's	they'd
let's	have	I'm

are family	had/would family
not family	will family

aren't	couldn't	I'd
isn't	wasn't	haven't
he'd	you'd	they'll
you'll	we're	we'll
they're	doesn't	hasn't
can't	shouldn't	it'll
who'd	there'd	they'd
that'll	don't	weren't
you're	she'd	I'll
he'll	hadn't	she'll

is/has family	*have* family
us family	*am* family	*will* family

---

let's	we've	it's
I'll	should've	here's
he's	that'll	she'll
who's	that's	she's
it'll	would've	you've
they've	there's	he'll
what's	I've	we'll
could've	you'll	they'll
there'll	where's	when's
I'm	how's	why's

am family	*are* family	*had/would* family	*have* family
is/has family	*not* family	*us* family	*will* family

- -

wouldn't	it'll	who'd
you've	they've	that'll
doesn't	there'd	we're
who's	what's	I'll
I'm	he'll	isn't
let's	we'd	don't
he'd	she'll	hasn't
they're	can't	how's
I've	they'd	haven't
here's	wasn't	weren't

am family	are family	have family	is/has family	had/would family
not family	us family	will family		**OUT OF SORTS**

wouldn't	they've	let's
here's	you'd	shell
I'll	you're	could've
they're	don't	hadn't
she'd	hasn't	he'd
we've	it'll	cannot
wasn't	he's	weren't
I'm	where's	she's
who's	could	what's
isn't	how's	went

contractions

compound words

cannot	lighthouse	we'll
can't	she'd	stairway
without	shouldn't	could've
he's	sunlight	they've
they're	bedroom	here's
isn't	where's	newscast
flagpole	baseball	mailbox
handprint	that'll	it's
you'll	couldn't	cornhusk
that's	he'll	aren't

contractions
compound words

landmark	could've	birdbath
popcorn	seafood	should've
we'd	hairbrush	outdoors
daylight	you'll	hasn't
we're	lifeguard	weren't
she'll	toothpaste	herself
I've	football	they'd
where's	it's	he's
couldn't	they're	raindrop
lifetime	airplane	you're

contractions	compound words
	OUT OF SORTS

cupcake	I'm	houseboat
that'll	windpipe	you'll
business	would've	boat
wherever	otherwise	don't
can't	house	we'll
she'll	cupboard	she'd
cannot	there's	hillside
shouldn't	let's	teapot
weren't	isn't	they'll
runway	happy	sailboat

double the final consonant	don't double the final consonant

---

fan	rain	roar
tip	keep	rub
cheer	drop	dip
hug	mark	win
push	beg	chew
need	knit	hop
eat	net	can
fish	trip	hunt
spill	pad	fool
farm	stop	pet

double the final consonant	don't double the final consonant

drag	ship	step
melt	fill	chop
tip	call	blend
pat	net	slip
ask	quit	learn
twist	wreck	rob
scar	thin	jog
pin	jump	fool
hiss	munch	snap
knot	drop	seal

drop the final *e*	don't drop the final *e*

- -

shade	flame	pipe
dare	clean	point
comb	like	smell
miss	file	store
bake	save	smile
cross	heal	gain
name	place	ride
push	farm	ice
note	pull	loan
grade	lift	stamp

drop the final e	don't drop the final e

march	trade	thin
point	rob	save
stamp	owe	chime
grade	chase	plan
strive	pipe	race
tune	star	ride
shape	want	note
speed	help	pad
pile	shop	make
mine	flame	price

double the final consonant	drop the final *e*

pin	trap	rob
knot	care	fan
take	dare	like
trip	smile	scar
file	pet	store
tame	pad	hope
score	chop	hop
snap	shake	slip
mop	line	use
chase	blame	sob

double the final consonant	drop the final e

sob	blame	pin
thin	drag	score
skate	file	like
fume	knit	mop
trap	chime	note
trade	fan	star
slip	bat	line
ship	race	net
save	hope	jog
ice	plug	mine

double the final consonant	drop the final e	**OUT OF SORTS**

wave	trap	tame
tug	shade	knot
smile	jog	slope
step	dare	line
race	shake	ship
shout	nest	drop
stare	scoop	grade
hope	slip	save
bake	price	grab
mark	care	wag

double the final consonant	no change / drop the e

make	shut	rip
sag	sip	drop
stop	hide	bump
shout	slant	smile
moan	blind	snack
hunt	pelt	smell
wed	move	slap
vote	stripe	hop
drip	heal	hope
seat	snake	grade

double the final consonant	no change
	drop the e

fan	wave	double
pin	ship	slump
slope	glide	bead
step	miss	heat
tap	vote	fool
tape	dot	scold
hook	milk	clap
shop	melt	hint
grip	duck	name
plan	sift	tune

CVC pattern with short vowels	CVCC pattern with short vowels

jump	cash	pan
hop	then	lift
clip	pit	fin
drag	task	rob
miss	pill	pen
run	pick	stop
wink	hit	ten
milk	fan	send
melt	miss	wet
lock	jog	fix

CVC pattern with short vowels	CVVC pattern with long vowels

weep	wait	tap
hop	net	can
fail	pop	cheer
lip	claim	trail
loan	roar	heat
speak	step	fit
need	tug	gain
pad	groan	pet
rub	seam	jeep
seal	cheek	hug

VCCV pattern	VCCV pattern
no doubled consonant	doubled consonant

helmet	elbow	slipper
letter	fabric	soccer
village	worry	person
yellow	copper	pencil
husband	coffee	gallows
picnic	reptile	plastic
traffic	pardon	winter
comment	orbit	passage
button	spelling	wedding
sudden	blossom	funny

first syllable stressed	second syllable stressed

navy	panic	figure
atom	prepare	habit
beyond	raccoon	unite
police	pretend	prison
super	repair	lily
dessert	although	propel
dozen	deny	comic
spinach	elect	siren
cartoon	select	pony
hotel	forget	camel

first syllable stressed	second syllable stressed

album	pollute	prevent
obey	remain	pilgrim
walrus	puddle	polite
beside	seldom	event
severe	carpet	reveal
comfort	complete	children
decide	orbit	temper
cement	market	debate
chili	midget	enjoy
cactus	morning	habit

al	aw
au	

bald	vault	drawn
haunch	lawn	walk
draw	straw	yawn
false	pawn	cause
gnaw	mall	gauze
call	sauce	salt
taught	scald	chalk
waltz	shawl	thaw
launch	malt	fraud
crawl	fawn	dawn

al	aw
au	

caught	scald	cause
bawl	small	claw
balk	sprawl	false
salt	jaw	hauled
haunt	waltz	haunch
ball	chalk	halt
hawk	gnaw	slaw
fraud	drawn	launch
raw	stalk	crawl
shawl	sauce	stall

al	aw
au	**OUT OF SORTS**

---

caw	haunt	full
cause	draw	bald
drawl	melt	sauce
lawn	scald	fawn
squawk	stall	frown
clown	raw	false
taught	fraud	wall
called	thaw	crawl
sprawl	halt	malt
yawn	small	bawl

| add *s* | add *es* |

box	nurse	gas
cow	leash	braid
witch	label	guess
string	inch	exam
bath	dish	six
arch	siren	boss
apple	adult	street
tulip	latch	brush
tax	square	lunch
puzzle	beach	index

add *s*	add *es*

bush	judge	flash
fox	batch	parent
result	class	ash
rule	rich	sleeve
bunch	index	crash
loss	pass	finch
peach	riddle	shadow
bonus	horn	atlas
tax	dish	cross
horse	latch	pebble

add *s*	add *es*

OUT OF SORTS

base	spice	wire
class	latch	bush
deer	exam	peach
bunch	kiss	woman
push	brush	actor
ruler	sheep	ash
bonus	mitten	coin
adult	pass	oxen
inch	rich	fish
box	lynx	geese

add *s*	add *es*
change *y* to *i* and add *es*	

dish	atlas	jelly
badge	arch	six
bully	berry	batch
notch	city	gas
class	inch	daisy
leash	country	chair
tax	wagon	army
robot	push	sky
party	lunch	seat
mass	guess	pony

add *s*	add *es*
change *y* to *i* and add *es*	

---

penny	bunny	arch
hitch	index	toss
train	teacher	inch
copy	acorn	leash
cross	jury	body
cabin	baby	watch
lily	beach	string
crash	iris	glass
fox	pass	ax
gas	lady	dragon

add *s*	add *es*	OUT OF SORTS

change *y* to *i* and add *es*

dress	push	bath
mix	medal	pass
bump	man	match
hill	crash	ruby
calf	park	atlas
chick	daisy	bench
trophy	elf	county
lunch	crayon	cousin
sheep	fox	glass
bus	hitch	cry

add *s*	add *es*	**OUT OF SORTS**

change *y* to *i* and add *es*

---

path	country	man
dress	spy	kiss
brush	mix	fish
fly	class	buggy
inch	posy	index
pastry	notch	bush
bunch	hitch	sheep
sneeze	trouser	rich
bus	deer	woman
ax	ruler	lady

open syllable (long vowel sound)	closed syllable (short vowel sound)

credit	siren	atom
spoken	sofa	camel
jacket	pony	figure
music	lemon	dozen
timid	honey	shiny
unit	robot	solar
habit	comic	decade
label	honor	spicy
civil	ripen	novel
closet	digit	never

open syllable
closed syllable

- -

lizard	pony	travel
solo	navy	solid
zebra	figure	music
lemon	vanish	spoken
credit	lever	unit
tulip	edit	menu
ruby	comic	honey
spinach	ripen	govern
timid	pupil	frigid
radar	pilot	soda

open syllable
closed syllable

evil	female	image
item	china	siren
legend	comet	driven
money	finish	olive
program	level	novel
closet	solar	super
pirate	widen	habit
spicy	vacant	profile
cocoa	frigid	major
flavor	decade	crater

open syllable	OUT OF SORTS
closed syllable	

taxi	legend	grand
profit	gravel	atom
ripen	finish	frequent
speed	clever	glider
future	chili	olive
fever	super	moods
honest	baby	rumor
camel	bacon	troll
pupil	civil	tuna
photo	final	robot

open syllable with the VCV pattern	closed syllable with the VCCV pattern

paper	perform	vacant
student	cartoon	robot
forbid	admit	excite
before	spicy	confess
super	radar	indeed
decide	pirate	observe
ignore	discuss	ruby
enjoy	until	pony
tulip	dentist	confuse
label	widen	enter

open syllable with the VCV pattern	closed syllable with the VCCV pattern

custom	compass	final
index	basket	tulip
lazy	female	album
baby	basic	chimney
enter	dolphin	favor
legal	elbow	famous
fabric	even	expert
husband	cozy	contest
helmet	engine	garden
furnish	center	Friday

aCe	ai	ay
open syllable long a		

painter	prayer	skater
raisin	safety	sailor
parade	today	sayings
rabies	refrain	grayish
nation	graceful	exclaim
maybe	shaky	behave
contain	dainty	baseball
embrace	engrave	drainage
sacred	raining	lazy
vapor	cradle	dismay

aCe	ai	ay
open syllable long a		

- -

player	skateboard	rabies
basil	graceful	mailboxes
crayfish	payment	engrave
erase	savor	statement
tailor	await	nation
remain	estate	daylight
failure	exclaim	railroad
maybe	decay	behave
astray	crater	betray
draining	daydream	wafer

aCe	ai	ay
open syllable long a		

---

explain	layer	data
savor	mainland	traitor
grapefruit	mistake	parade
sustain	pavement	fatal
shaky	raven	hooray
rainbow	raincoat	strainer
today	painful	cascade
decay	create	campaign
fable	bracelet	astray
nation	crayon	ladle

aCe	ai	ay	**OUT OF SORTS**

open syllable long a

navy	today	while
graying	complain	decay
grapevines	basement	mailman
lead	hatred	waiter
playful	motor	refrain
patient	shaky	April
rainy	glacier	graceful
snakebite	astray	escape
scrape	tailor	seeing
maybe	lakeside	pavement

ee	ea	ie

- -

repeal	eager	mislead
easy	release	sleeping
canteen	freeway	besiege
tureen	retrieve	defeat
believe	easel	cheetah
kneecap	conceal	apiece
diesel	breezy	beaver
indeed	relief	degree
agree	ideal	weasel
achieve	greeting	relieve

ee	ea	ie

---

brief	ordeal	diesel
freeway	besiege	achieve
steeply	greeting	degree
reveal	disease	breeze
relief	appeal	between
release	sweeping	retrieve
belief	peanut	greenish
redeem	meanwhile	steeple
baleen	indeed	relieve
eager	mislead	increase

ee	ea	ie

OUT OF SORTS

- -

gleeful	tweezers	blown
ideal	reveal	between
achieve	unseen	apiece
between	training	proceed
esteem	believe	peanut
relieve	ordeal	music
defeat	kneecap	disease
gated	freedom	cheaply
relief	mislead	sweeping
eager	besiege	meanwhile

eCe	ei
open syllable long e	

- -

delete	supreme	receipt
either	deplete	meter
sequence	neither	extreme
prefix	fever	leisure
even	species	precede
caffeine	perceive	serene
compete	ceiling	seizure
tepees	discrete	recent
zebra	legal	depot
receive	recede	cedar

eCe	ei
open syllable long e	

- -

secede	species	conceive
delete	legal	recent
receive	decent	impede
detour	receipt	replete
veto	ceiling	either
neither	discrete	convene
deceive	concede	female
meter	fever	serene
regal	preview	stampede
complete	leisure	caffeine

eCe	ei	**OUT OF SORTS**
open syllable long e		

---

ceiling	complete	seizure
smell	detour	discrete
prefix	trapeze	perceive
deplete	convene	regal
either	receipt	female
smart	replete	supreme
recede	delete	leisure
legal	choose	tuned
fever	secede	serene
receive	neither	caffeine

iCe	igh	iCC
open syllable long i		y

advise	defy	sidewalk
binder	dryer	tighten
tonight	lighten	pirate
typist	iceberg	dining
remind	childish	rewind
biker	wildcat	divide
sightsee	spider	fighter
dislike	visor	flyer
highway	climber	July
diner	invite	title

iCe	igh	iCC
open syllable long i		y

unkind	icy	wildlife
writer	bypass	flighty
tyrant	binder	finely
nighttime	highway	dryer
widely	delight	bridle
surprise	decide	climber
mighty	highness	driveway
findings	blindfold	resign
hydrant	nylon	nightmare
rhino	rival	sinus

iCe	igh	iCC
open syllable long i		y

- -

bison	stylish	survive
apply	design	recline
assign	sightsee	imply
highway	ninety	spyglass
lightning	iceberg	kindness
excite	rhyming	gyro
confide	miser	delight
lighthouse	cider	pliers
rely	bindings	remind
item	tonight	unkind

iCe	igh	iCC	y
open syllable long i			**OUT OF SORTS**

remind	assign	waiting
mighty	rhyme	timer
even	despite	hybrid
minus	leave	item
ignite	oblige	rewind
invite	dining	delight
highway	findings	trapped
python	refine	climber
slimy	sightless	gyro
diver	provide	tripod

oCe	oa	oCC
open syllable long o		**ow**

arose	revolt	goldfinch
cobra	crowbar	snowflake
polka	pony	coastal
roadway	tollbooth	glowworm
unload	soldier	soda
homework	stroller	ocean
poster	rowers	notice
snowshoe	motor	goalie
donate	explode	enclose
lonely	lonesome	protein

oCe	oa	oCC
open syllable long o		ow

rodent	erode	moment
snowshoe	dispose	frozen
withhold	foretold	coldness
roadside	odor	coaching
coastal	local	rotate
coleslaw	almost	disown
goalie	coattail	revolt
potion	boathouse	toadstool
molding	enroll	soapy
sofa	lower	hopeful

oCe	oa	oCC
open syllable long o		ow

awoke	coaster	homeless
approach	coldness	moldings
almost	snowfall	snowshoe
aglow	social	moment
hopeful	cobra	locate
uphold	hostess	nomad
loafer	program	postcard
explode	bestow	coastal
notion	roadway	goalie
enroll	erode	disown

oCe	oa	oCC	ow
open syllable long o			**OUT OF SORTS**

pronoun	goldfinch	aglow
motor	smoky	disown
owner	grocer	floating
molten	bowling	homesick
postage	behold	boots
plot	awake	toaster
notebook	rosebush	almost
afloat	approach	pinned
smolder	hotel	explode
snowball	donate	hotter

uCe	open syllable long u

---

lukewarm	reduce	humid
ruling	conclude	pollute
pupil	tunic	truly
amuse	human	super
jukebox	futile	consume
student	humor	tuna
tumor	dilute	future
misuse	exclude	excuse
confuse	bugle	tutor
rumor	include	resume

uCe	open syllable long u

sumac	confuse	super
ruby	include	human
compute	tuba	future
conclude	futile	tuna
rumor	tulip	protrude
exclude	perfume	salute
abuse	tumor	tubeless
bugle	ruling	lukewarm
humid	amuse	student
truly	reduce	music

uCe	open syllable long u

---

abuse	tuna	resume
bugle	rumor	tulip
tutor	dispute	ruling
yuletide	dilute	music
acute	pupil	exclude
futile	lukewarm	humor
future	excuse	sumac
compute	truly	confuse
include	ruby	salute
student	humid	tumor

uCe	open syllable long u

OUT OF SORTS

tutor	pupil	humid
yuletide	excuse	ugly
useful	dispute	include
suture	center	dungeon
preclude	tulip	super
reduce	planning	misuse
rumor	salute	music
ruby	ruling	protrude
presume	truly	tunic
lukewarm	resume	tuba

short a	aCe	ai
ay	open syllable a	

gallop	lantern	mainland
radar	engrave	persuade
disgrace	raincoat	basis
failure	mayor	grayish
hammer	today	portray
prayer	railroad	massive
complain	erase	sailor
behave	cannon	nation
debate	estate	await
satin	scatter	lazy

short a	aCe	ai
ay	open syllable a	

rainbow	ambush	fable
flashlight	payment	maybe
persuade	create	basic
safety	trainer	mailbox
sayings	parade	agent
crayon	okay	daddy
failure	drainage	debate
crater	bracelet	portray
engage	canvas	painter
expand	lazy	skateboard

short a	aCe long a	ai long a
ay long a	open syllable long a	**OUT OF SORTS**

---

patent	speeder	betray
safety	radar	acquaint
rainbow	lazy	cattle
cartoon	baseball	maybe
basement	amaze	smiling
playmate	rabies	layer
daydream	shook	banter
okay	strainer	skater
expand	nation	tailor
ranch	bracelet	mistake

short e	short ea	long ee	long ea
long ie	open syllable long e	long eCe	long ei

compete	belief	eager
being	cheaply	connects
receive	redeem	exit
heavy	ordeal	ready
agree	believe	peanut
appeal	serene	succeed
achieve	receipt	leather
event	prefix	relief
deafen	either	cedar
degree	trapeze	ceiling

short e	short ea	long ee	long ea
long ie	open syllable long e	long eCe	long ei

seizure	steady	reveal
female	distress	connect
impede	beggar	delete
neither	dreadful	species
greeting	asleep	stampede
ideal	sweeten	perceive
heavy	release	legal
feather	healthy	relieve
creature	retrieve	defeat
relief	cheetah	freedom

short e	short ea	long ee	long ea	long ie
open syllable long e	long eCe	long ei	OUT OF SORTS

confess	beaver	between
greenish	receive	plated
pheasant	caffeine	supreme
eager	tureen	decent
apiece	snoring	leisure
heavy	acorn	pinned
effect	debrief	treasure
convene	ready	seedling
precede	elect	creature
meter	attend	achieve

| short i | y short i | iCe long i | igh long i |

| iCC long i | y long i | open syllable long i |

nightmare	invite	hydrant
wildcat	mighty	simmer
precise	blindfold	physics
pirate	July	sinus
apply	rival	python
sightsee	fighter	insect
decline	behind	rhythm
unkind	divide	opinion
lively	gypsy	iris
remind	gyro	cider

short i	y short i	iCe long i	igh long i

iCC long i	y long i	open syllable long i

wildcat	highway	pliers
lighten	despite	rely
cyclist	gypsy	minus
dinner	dryer	assign
physics	slimy	ninety
sightsee	tripod	ignite
pillow	insect	symbol
rifle	invite	illness
flyer	arrive	sizzle
findings	bindings	supply

short i	y short i	iCe long i	igh long i
iCC long i	y long i	open syllable long i	**OUT OF SORTS**

ribbon	enlist	purple
system	index	cymbal
nylon	gypsy	lightning
wildcat	cartoon	imply
rhythm	dining	pirate
climber	invite	childhood
flyer	sightsee	delight
rival	defy	needless
title	icy	visor
sightless	street	flying

short o	oCe long o	oa long o
oCC long o	ow long o	open syllable long o

honest	novel	roadway
afloat	uphold	notebook
explode	rowers	soapy
polka	crowbar	floating
snowstorm	local	notice
soda	homework	trophy
pony	cobwebs	toaster
soldier	propose	chopstick
unload	poster	profit
copper	lower	total

short o	oCe long o	oa long o
oCC long o	ow long o	open syllable long o

---

forgot	rowing	decode
pocket	tollbooth	coastline
boater	lobby	showdown
snowman	modern	postman
odor	owner	loafer
moment	toadstool	social
lonesome	rotten	goalie
roadway	awoke	poster
enroll	frozen	stovepipe
below	sofa	homesick

short o	oCe long o	oa long o

oCC long o	ow long o	open syllable long o	**OUT OF SORTS**

snowball	lonely	folktales
unload	respond	boathouse
erode	battle	notion
robber	snowfall	soapy
driver	locate	lonesome
postage	painting	spoken
coattail	rowing	forgot
total	problem	bottle
poster	splatter	reblown
toaster	chopstick	hopeful

short u	uCe long u

open syllable long u

- -

punish	husband	jukebox
tunic	cluster	publish
presume	erupt	fumble
rugged	reduce	rumor
tulip	truly	pupil
human	music	confuse
dilute	hundred	funny
salute	humid	dispute
future	excuse	jungle
compute	grumpy	tuna

short u	uCe long u
open syllable long u	

thunder	fumble	perfume
resume	pumpkin	truly
tutor	acute	mustard
sumac	humor	rumor
mustang	bugle	abuse
publish	instruct	tuna
excuse	yuletide	include
conclude	clumsy	tumor
student	dilute	jukebox
music	snuggle	rustle

short u	uCe long u
open syllable long u	**OUT OF SORTS**

pollute	erupt	disgust
ruling	super	misuse
instruct	bugle	excuse
apple	trained	humor
fumble	public	human
reduce	rugged	custom
tumor	pupil	exclude
futile	moved	student
hundred	thousand	amuse
distrust	rumor	chuckle

| ar (as in *marker*) | are |
| ar (as in *narrate*) | air |

vary	prepare	compare
hairpin	parsley	tardy
rarest	narrow	carriage
parkway	dairy	prairie
cartwheel	barely	party
sparrow	marrow	parent
airport	barefoot	airwaves
declare	parka	repair
marble	charter	spareribs
garnet	tariff	aircraft

| ar (as in *marke*r) | are |
| ar (as in *narrate*) | air |

larva	garland	aware
garlic	narrate	sarcasm
warehouse	declare	prepare
fairground	marriage	parent
carol	haircut	farmhouse
airmail	beware	harvest
carefree	aircraft	despair
marshal	carrot	careful
apart	fairway	tariff
darkness	airlines	barren

ar (as in *marker*)	are	OUT OF
ar (as in *narrate*)	air	SORTS

marrow	meeting	starchy
chairman	stairway	bareback
compare	barrel	margin
parcel	partner	alive
opinion	barber	farther
repair	narrate	scarab
parish	affair	dairy
parrot	declare	spareribs
rarely	initial	barracks
cartridge	staircase	prepare

er	**ere**	**eer**
ear (as in *heard*)		**ear** (as in *fear*)

- -

perfect	severe	derrick
unearned	yearning	person
veneer	jersey	peering
revere	dreary	sincere
gearshift	merely	adhere
appear	sheerest	searchlight
herdsman	career	dearest
verbal	relearn	deerskin
prefer	early	earthen
berry	nervous	fearful

er	ere	eer

ear (as in *heard*)	ear (as in *fear*)

---

steerage	leery	teardrop
hereby	appear	deerskin
learner	early	merely
relearn	herbal	peering
gerbil	severe	reverse
thermos	clearing	austere
merry	dearest	research
sermon	rehearse	cheerful
unearned	yearning	mermaid
earthquake	perky	cashmere

er	ere	eer	**OUT OF SORTS**

ear (as in *heard*)	**ear** (as in *fear*)

sincere	leery	deerskin
sheerest	kerchief	dearest
fearful	research	bearded
clearing	hermit	pearly
learner	nonsense	jumping
reserve	witness	yearning
earthworm	revere	adhere
penpal	tearful	spearhead
jeering	unearned	yearbook
nearby	perfect	hereby

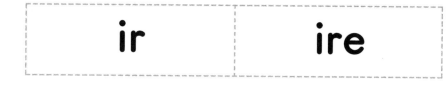

dirty	rehire	sirloin
perspire	firefly	whirlwind
girlfriend	attire	birthday
twirler	tiredness	expire
require	inquire	firehouse
tiresome	whirlpool	fireproof
circle	shirttail	firmly
birdhouse	skirmish	desire
irksome	retire	confirm
circus	afire	wiretap

perspire	expire	tiresome
inquire	fireplace	entire
acquire	twirler	dirty
circuit	chirping	sirloin
astir	birthmark	desire
attire	fireproof	retire
flirting	admire	fireman
irksome	girlfriend	firmly
whirlpool	thirsty	swirling
rehire	inspire	circle

ir	ire

OUT OF SORTS

---

firmly	chirping	whirlpool
virtue	aspire	flirting
inquire	entire	retire
sitting	admire	perspire
fireproof	liter	birdseed
tiresome	birdbath	physical
expire	birthstone	directions
answer	fireman	inspire
circuit	direful	confirm
affirm	rehire	irksome

or	ore
oar	our

torchlight	story	boarding
adore	restore	courtyard
aboard	shoreline	hoarding
courthouse	coarsely	snorkel
sources	fourteen	floral
yourself	forty	forfeit
hoarsely	torrent	fortress
ignore	storeroom	horseback
shortcake	before	explore
cornstarch	boardwalk	mournful

or	ore
oar	our

aboard	hoarseness	restore
coarseness	pouring	boredom
courtyard	foursome	sources
storefront	boarding	fourteen
adore	coarsely	boardwalk
shortage	torment	tortoise
corner	cornstarch	sportsman
border	forfeit	corking
porridge	forceful	forging
shoreline	cornmeal	galore

or	ore	OUT OF
oar	our	SORTS

- -

hoarseness	shortcake	boardroom
shook	ignore	snorkel
aboard	coarsely	corncob
fourteen	mournful	fierceness
stormy	restore	pouring
torchlight	bookroom	sorrow
porthole	portrait	deplore
before	ashore	coarseness
storeroom	scoreless	porpoise
shorebird	courtship	courtroom

ur	ure

---

burglar	further	furnace
surgeon	surefire	purebred
assure	obscure	turkey
unsure	impure	mature
flurry	turnstile	turnip
turtle	bursting	curfew
surely	curbstone	obscure
endure	procure	ensure
cursor	turban	brochure
curtain	plural	secure

ur	ure

curtain	curry	purebred
furnish	mature	endure
turnip	assure	cursive
currant	Thursday	burden
burly	hurdle	furrow
impure	procure	surrey
surefire	turquoise	pressure
turret	brochure	surgeon
unsure	curvy	surely
surplus	jury	secure

ur	ure

OUT OF SORTS

- -

purple	curtain	turtle
furrow	rural	hurry
secure	shaken	burden
jersey	juror	surefire
flute	unsure	assure
turret	hurdle	murder
mature	gurgle	brochure
curfew	impure	insane
burglar	surplus	during
obscure	ensure	endure

oo (as in *food*)   **ew**

oo (as in *foot*)

- -

aloof	poodle	shampoo
noodle	footprints	rookie
cookbook	pewter	dewdrop
woodland	renew	footage
toothache	moody	steward
raccoon	cookout	anew
skewer	cartoon	sooty
chewy	lagoon	maroon
football	cashew	bassoon
harpoon	woodpile	foothills

oo (as in *food*)	ew

| oo (as in *foot*) | |

---

woodwind	aloof	dewdrop
rooster	woodland	woodchuck
bookworm	pewter	footage
chewy	cashew	kazoo
mistook	crewman	cartoon
jewel	footprints	baboon
monsoon	doodle	skewer
bookshelf	cocoon	rookie
cookout	askew	noodle
bassoon	cookbook	balloon

oy	oi
ou	ow

royal	county	drowsy
mousetrap	exploit	counter
counsel	soybean	voyage
allow	doubtful	rejoice
towel	cowhand	destroy
profound	blower	foundry
enjoy	devour	employ
doily	oyster	coward
poison	mountain	rowdy
endow	avoid	boycott

oy	oi
ou	ow

vowel	counsel	royal
rejoice	fountain	scoundrel
loyal	poison	oyster
council	voyage	drowsy
mouthwash	tower	bounty
dowry	devour	exploit
chowder	employ	doily
loiter	shower	ahoy
joyful	downfall	mountain
boycott	moisture	prowler

ew	oy	oi	ou
oo (as in *foot*)	**oo** (as in *food*)		**ow**

cartoon	rowdy	poison
destroy	football	skewer
bookcase	harpoon	rejoice
exploit	moody	doubtful
drowsy	annoy	powder
footage	woodwind	chowder
raccoon	moisture	loyal
crewman	enjoy	brownie
anew	pewter	appoint
fountain	jewel	profound

ew	oy	oi	ou
oo (as in *foot*)	**oo** (as in *food*)		**ow**

trowel	flower	tower
footprints	dewdrop	profound
joyful	moody	askew
bounty	mouthwash	shampoo
lagoon	rookie	jewel
chewy	noodle	mistook
toothache	bookcase	foundry
employ	loyal	enjoy
cookbook	moisture	boycott
voyage	appoint	anew

ain	an	en

in	on

given	resin	penguin
tartan	button	captain
villain	warden	falcon
aspen	airman	urban
barren	bargain	mitten
basin	certain	organ
apron	treason	prison
yeoman	turban	urchin
darken	wagon	caldron
swollen	garden	curtain

ain	an	en
in	on	

---

thicken	deafen	glutton
siren	muslin	strengthen
human	carton	organ
mountain	villain	certain
muffin	chicken	spoken
goblin	iron	bison
sultan	bacon	cousin
chaplain	seaman	kitten
children	chieftain	orphan
yeoman	bargain	fountain

al	il	ile
	el	le

---

weasel	parcel	towel
stencil	futile	hostile
sterile	fragile	spiral
plural	model	neutral
twinkle	global	April
medal	pedal	purple
fossil	evil	nostril
bagel	hazel	normal
beagle	bubble	missile
needle	pickle	bottle

al	il	ile

el	le

---

wrinkle	beetle	eagle
cuddle	bushel	cackle
panel	bridle	flannel
missile	docile	pencil
tranquil	lentil	normal
petal	crystal	central
plural	loyal	middle
fragile	struggle	squirrel
nostril	mammal	signal
diesel	tonsil	mumble

ar	er
or	

- -

skater	governor	altar
cylinder	armor	dollar
editor	hangar	splendor
peculiar	cougar	favor
molar	burglar	scooter
grammar	banner	vapor
tremor	consumer	fender
doctor	tweezers	mirror
lever	director	cheddar
founder	pillar	sugar

ar	er
or	

blister	emperor	singular
beginner	equator	lunar
circular	coaster	shopper
cougar	trooper	polar
surveyor	molar	nectar
visitor	dreamer	vendor
reader	meteor	traitor
cellar	cheaper	planner
burglar	ledger	jogger
fiercer	founder	briar

dis (opposite of)   **en** (to put into, make)

in (in or into)   **fore** (before, in front of)

- -

foresee	disclose	disregard
insight	encode	forearm
distrust	income	inland
forehead	inboard	disinfect
infield	indent	foremost
enforce	engulf	discharge
disfigure	disorder	enable
forehand	foreshadow	enact
enjoin	foresight	inflame
inseam	dishonest	enlist

dis (opposite of)   **en** (to put into, make)

in (in or into)   **fore** (before, in front of)

engulf	enfold	foresight
forerunner	disloyal	inlaid
enjoy	encase	foremost
dishonest	enslave	enlist
enable	disinfect	entomb
disable	disarm	disregard
foresight	inmate	endear
enroll	distaste	disorder
inboard	forehead	inset
income	disfavor	input

dis (opposite of)	**in** (in or into)	**OUT OF SORTS**
en (to put into, make)	**fore** (before, in front of)	

discover	discomfort	foreman
foremost	foreleg	insight
entrust	reject	dislike
misplace	engulf	indoors
unjust	disobey	forethought
foreclose	preview	inside
enlarge	ensnare	income
disfavor	disclose	enrich
endear	foresight	inland
enrage	disappear	input

mis (wrong)	pre (before)
re (again)	un (not, opposite of)

remodel	relearn	misgivings
unselfish	unnamed	reelect
unfreeze	misplace	reclaim
preview	premature	unequal
mismatch	mismanage	unleash
mistrust	relocate	preschool
pretest	uneven	miscount
unlike	unafraid	preexisting
unfair	predawn	readjust
refill	predate	recycle

mis (wrong)	pre (before)
re (again)	un (not, opposite of)

reform	unbeaten	pregame
undone	mishandle	misbehave
mistake	preshrunk	refresh
premix	misprint	unhappy
misspell	unfair	rephrase
redirect	mislead	uncooked
precook	reconstruct	misfire
reorder	unaware	unbroken
uncommon	reenact	refocus
rebound	prejudge	misuse

mis (wrong)	pre (before)	**OUT OF SORTS**
re (again)	un (not, opposite of)	

preset	reshape	misdeal
misguide	prepay	perfect
research	unafraid	rewrite
unfold	unnoticed	recycle
sharpness	refinish	precut
coolness	unbutton	remind
recopy	unable	spoonful
misinform	presoak	misgivings
prefix	mistaken	preheat
mislead	unlock	pretest

er (more)	**est** (most)
ful (full of, having)	**less** (without)

speechless	helpful	quieter
nearer	plainer	warmest
powerful	friendless	thoughtful
oddest	darker	helpless
hopeful	boldest	meaningless
careless	endless	roughest
painless	playful	louder
lawful	firmer	quickest
wordless	cheerful	harmful
driest	colder	cleaner

er (more)	est (most)
ful (full of, having)	less (without)

---

smaller	sweeter	colorful
mouthful	tasteful	stressful
limitless	cloudless	timeless
meaningful	rougher	loudest
dearest	helpless	cheapest
peaceful	priceless	nearer
homeless	harder	jobless
youthful	quietest	wishful
fuller	bottomless	breathless
blacker	armful	doubtful

er (more)	est (most)	OUT OF SORTS
ful (full of, having)	less (without)	

sweeter	mismatch	meanest
odorless	limitless	brighter
faultless	thankless	truthful
firmest	uncommon	endless
preview	fairest	recapture
powerful	spoonful	playful
mouthful	speechless	clearest
armless	wasteful	cleanest
boastful	painless	cleaner
darker	graceful	stronger

ly (like, in a manner)   **ness** (state of being)

y (having)

---

badly	openness	sugary
awareness	tasty	weakness
dressy	moistness	cowardly
lately	eagerly	stiffness
needy	really	chilly
quietly	sharpness	legally
rusty	sandy	likely
distinctly	crispy	firmness
speedy	greasy	snowy
gladly	ripeness	thinness

ly (like, in a manner)	ness (state of being)

y (having)

noisy	weariness	loyally
heavily	safely	ripeness
lately	ugliness	dressy
readiness	gloomily	choppy
greedily	curly	hastily
deadly	stormy	rudely
vastness	moistness	stillness
strangely	directly	coolness
windy	skinny	worthy
hungrily	busily	gladness

ly (like, in a manner)   **ness** (state of being)

y (having)   **OUT OF SORTS**

happiness	finally	haziness
daintily	filthy	awareness
easily	react	unnoticed
bumpy	fondness	weakness
goodness	gritty	legally
tasteless	costly	fuzziness
deeply	scariness	thirsty
bravely	wishful	crudely
choppy	equally	rainy
shortly	dusty	foggy

c	que	ke
k	ck	

---

turnpike	public	keepsake
zodiac	tonic	bedrock
fabric	oarlock	provoke
network	crosswalk	brusque
homesick	forsake	gimmick
shellac	opaque	mistake
Pacific	classic	torque
slowpoke	hallmark	stick
derrick	potluck	artwork
evoke	plaque	unique

c	que	ke
k	ck	

slowpoke	cupcake	critique
toxic	antique	hallmark
hammock	poetic	namesake
landmark	ethnic	carsick
pancake	hassock	mistake
clique	cornstalk	plaque
rustic	earthquake	tactic
cosmic	boutique	benchmark
cowlick	tropic	bedrock
berserk	dynamic	picnic

c	que	ke
k	ck	**OUT OF SORTS**

oarlock	embark	physique
bisque	keeping	namesake
scenic	homework	curtain
fetlock	comic	organic
paddock	cubic	forsake
kitchen	gimmick	clambake
oblique	cassock	baroque
ransack	haddock	frantic
dynamic	tragic	earmark
seasick	relic	kept

se, te—drop *e* and add *ion*

de—drop *de* and add *sion*

frustrate	incise	decide
frustration	incision	decision
provide	revise	include
provision	revision	inclusion
supervise	conclude	delude
supervision	conclusion	delusion
create	dictate	corrode
creation	dictation	corrosion
complete	allude	anticipate
completion	allusion	anticipation
tense	collide	appreciate
tension	collision	appreciation
invade	hesitate	persuade
invasion	hesitation	persuasion
fuse	repulse	abbreviate
fusion	repulsion	abbreviation
evade	precise	protrude
evasion	precision	protrusion
celebrate	pretense	seclude
celebration	pretension	seclusion

> # se, te–drop *e* and add *ion*
>
> # de–drop *de* and add *sion*

transfuse transfusion	conclude conclusion	navigate navigation
televise television	operate operation	illustrate illustration
invade invasion	migrate migration	deride derision
delude delusion	confuse confusion	collide collision
evade evasion	circulate circulation	abrade abrasion
divide division	revise revision	provide provision
imitate imitation	include inclusion	pretense pretension
hibernate hibernation	fuse fusion	decorate decoration
evaporate evaporation	explode explosion	seclude seclusion
intrude intrusion	decide decision	translate translation

add *able* to base word

add *ible* to root word

prefer	pay	leg
terr	invinc	approach
reason	ed	ostens
question	credit	dirig
transfer	favor	compat
mand	irasc	expand
indel	gull	cred
depend	aud	laugh
tang	detest	agree
commend	adapt	cruc

add *able* to base word

add *ible* to root word

remark	plaus	detest
perish	vis	allow
feas	respect	plaus
cred	gull	poss
season	elig	aud
predict	ed	refill
tang	punish	fashion
incorrig	read	cruc
commend	irasc	compat
transfer	consider	reason

drop the *e*	drop the *ate*

change the *y* to *i*

pleasure	love	ply
certify	separate	debate
estimate	modify	advise
irritate	imitate	vegetate
remove	endure	appreciate
deny	size	observe
operate	pity	identify
excite	educate	envy
note	assume	penetrate
justify	tolerate	rely

drop the *e*	drop the *ate*

change the *y* to *i*

excite	recycle	dispose
achieve	rely	assume
vary	like	modify
venerate	negotiate	reuse
debate	quantify	deny
classify	oppose	observe
remedy	operate	envy
excuse	identify	desire
breathe	cultivate	ply
irritate	endure	note

double the final consonant	
do not double the final consonant	

emit	support	regret
detour	attend	forbid
admit	allot	appear
defer	forget	submit
control	refer	complain
exist	insert	confer
prevent	excel	acquit
begin	omit	explain
equip	collect	transfer
repeat	detour	regret

double the final consonant

do not double the final consonant

- -

complain	insert	equip
attend	rebel	exist
defer	forget	omit
acquit	support	allot
regret	conduct	permit
expel	propel	collect
confer	admit	patrol
explain	repeat	detour
control	refer	commit
prevent	appear	forbid

| change *sis* to *ses* | change *a* to *ae* |
| change *us* to *i* | change *um* to *a* |

basis	oasis	nucleus
alga	crisis	octopus
addendum	cirrus	medium
alumnus	stylus	synthesis
analysis	syllabus	antenna
nova	rhombus	diagnosis
cactus	curriculum	formula
datum	radius	vertebra
fungus	bacterium	focus
stratum	consortium	larva

change *sis* to *ses*	change *a* to *ae*
change *us* to *i*	change *um* to *a*

analysis	synopsis	fungus
alga	crisis	octopus
alumnus	persona	formula
thesaurus	cactus	nucleus
stratum	datum	curriculum
symposium	solarium	referendum
thesis	stimulus	nova
nemesis	radius	antenna
larva	oasis	addendum
bacterium	basis	vertebra

anti (against)	auto (self)
cat, cata (down)	circum (around)

automatic	autocrat	antipathy
catacomb	antitrust	catastrophe
circumfuse	catalogue	circumstance
automobile	autopsy	autobiography
circumvent	antifreeze	anticlimactic
antitoxin	circumpolar	circumspect
autograph	cataract	cataclysm
circumference	autonomy	antihistamine
catatonic	catapult	antidote
antiwar	antiseptic	automaton

anti (against)	**auto** (self)
cat, cata (down)	**circum** (around)

circumspect	circumference	circumnavigate
antipathy	catalepsy	circumpolar
antihistamine	antiseptic	catacomb
circumstance	antitrust	autograph
automaton	autocrat	circumfuse
catastrophe	catalogue	automobile
autobiography	automatic	circumvent
anticlimactic	catapult	autopsy
cataclysm	autonomy	antiwar
cataract	antifreeze	antipathy

anti (against)	**auto** (self)	**OUT OF SORTS**

cat, cata (down)	**circum** (around)

- -

antifreeze	catalogue	antitrust
circumvent	antisocial	autobiography
antihistamine	anticlimactic	catastrophe
automobile	circumstance	cataclysm
circumference	autonomy	postpone
transplant	catapult	cataract
autopsy	automatic	decade
antiwar	catacomb	circumfuse
automaton	malfunction	circumspect
autocrat	circumpolar	antibiotic

| **inter** (between, among) | **intra** (within) |
| **mal, male** (bad, evil) | **peri** (around, near) |

interact	malady	periodontal
intramural	perimeter	malefactor
maladjusted	malnutrition	malevolent
pericardium	interloper	interface
perigee	interlock	periscope
malpractice	malaria	interlace
intrastate	period	periphery
intermission	malfunction	interrupt
intercede	interject	malinger
intravenous	interchange	malign

inter (between, among)   **intra** (within)

mal, male (bad, evil)   **peri** (around, near)

malpractice	interloper	malcontent
peripatetic	intrastate	intravenous
maladjusted	malfunction	malign
pericardium	malfeasance	perigee
intramural	periphery	intermediary
interact	malady	periodontal
intermission	malefactor	malaria
period	interchange	interlock
periscope	intercollegiate	interface
intercede	perimeter	malnutrition

inter (between, among)   **mal, male** (bad, evil)

intra (within)   **peri** (around, near)   OUT OF SORTS

interloper	catapult	interpret
intrastate	interchange	period
malefactor	perimeter	perigee
circumvent	intermediary	intramural
intravenous	malfunction	maladjusted
malady	periscope	pericardium
malcontent	intercede	peripatetic
periodontal	intermission	malpractice
malaria	interact	malign
interlock	translate	autocrat

post (after)	pro (before, forward)
super (higher, greater)	trans (over, across)

- -

posterior	transplant	proficient
provide	supersonic	transfuse
transpose	transit	supersede
supervision	profane	superman
superficial	postpone	translate
proceed	superpower	postdate
posterity	profess	postdoctoral
supermarket	progress	program
transport	postmeridian	pronounce
proclaim	supernatural	postscript

post (after)	pro (before, forward)
super (higher, greater)	trans (over, across)

- -

postpone	transit	transcribe
proceed	profound	prohibit
proclaim	profile	transgress
transatlantic	postscript	superman
transpose	superstition	supersede
provide	transcend	supersonic
posterior	propel	transmit
supervision	transparent	posthumous
supercilious	progress	posterity
transfigure	prodigy	supermarket

post (after)   **pro** (before, forward)   **OUT OF SORTS**

super (higher, greater)   **trans** (over, across)

transfer	transport	superimpose
propel	superstition	superman
postscript	autograph	superficial
transatlantic	transplant	promote
transpose	supersonic	postdate
antitrust	proportion	posterity
proceed	postpone	prohibit
posterior	transpire	transgress
supervision	malaria	posthumous
proclaim	prophet	supersede

| bi (two) | dec, deca (ten) | mon, mono (one, alone) |
| oct, octo, octa (eight) | cent, centi (hundred) | multi (much, many) |

- -

octagon	multicolored	multifaceted
multitude	octillion	bimonthly
monotonous	multiple	centipede
decameter	monotone	December
centimeter	decimal	monolith
biweekly	bilateral	octave
centigrade	October	monorail
biennial	centennial	decimeter
decade	bilingual	biped
monarchy	monotheism	century

bi (two)	dec, deca (ten)	mon, mono (one, alone)
oct, octo, octa (eight)	cent, centi (hundred)	multi (much, many)

- -

octave	multiplex	centipede
multifamily	octagon	multiply
monologue	monastery	octopus
decade	December	multiple
century	bipartisan	monograph
bisect	bivalve	percent
multitude	centigrade	decameter
octahedron	monopoly	biped
bipolar	octet	monarchy
centimeter	monorail	decagon

bi (two)	dec, deca (ten)	mon, mono (one, alone)
oct, octo, octa (eight)	cent, centi (hundred)	multi (much, many)	**OUT OF SORTS**

- -

octet	centipede	multiplex
multitude	postpone	monologue
mountain	biped	centigrade
decade	centenarian	bipolar
century	decagon	decameter
supersonic	monograph	December
biweekly	multilateral	bimonthly
multiple	octahedron	October
octagon	octopus	monolith
monastery	monotone	biennial

pent, penta (five)	poly (many)	quad, quadri (four)
semi (half, partly)	tri (three)	uni (one)

- -

pentagon	quadrant	semitropical
polychrome	polytechnic	quadrille
triad	triplet	polysyllabic
semiannual	semicolon	pentatonic
quadrangle	triceps	quadruplets
unicorn	pentameter	uniform
tripod	polygon	unity
unicycle	semiyearly	universal
triangle	quadriceps	polyphonic
semicircle	trio	pentathlon

pent, penta (five)	poly (many)	quad, quadri (four)
semi (half, partly)	tri (three)	uni (one)

unit	polyphony	semicolon
trinity	triplet	unilateral
semisolid	unique	university
quadruple	semiyearly	semifinal
polynomial	quadrant	polygraph
pentagon	pentathlon	unison
triennial	semicircle	pentadactyl
pentameter	tricycle	polygon
semidetached	unicycle	unity
quadrille	Pentecost	quadruped

pent, penta (five)	poly (many)	quad, quadri (four)
semi (half, partly)	tri (three)	uni (one) / OUT OF SORTS

universe	polyphony	pentatonic
tripod	pentathlon	unison
semiweekly	unite	unilateral
quadruplets	trio	tricolor
polysyllabic	semisolid	semicircle
prophet	quadrille	polyhedron
universal	polynomial	bisect
triplet	pentameter	autograph
semiprivate	transport	semicolon
quadruped	quadriceps	pentagon

aer (air)	arch (chief, ruler)	aster (star)
bio (life)	centr (center)	cris, crit (to judge, separate)

crisis	criterion	architect
concentric	centrist	aerie
biology	critic	asteroid
astrophysics	biopsy	criticize
archduke	astrology	eccentric
aerate	archetype	biography
archangel	aerobic	symbiotic
asterisk	anarchy	critique
antibiotic	aerosol	aerobatics
astronaut	centrifugal	egocentric

chron (time)	**cycl** (circle)	**dem** (people)
derm (skin)	**geo** (earth)	**gram** (to write)

telegram	grammar	geothermal
taxidermy	epidermis	geology
democratic	geographic	hologram
tricycle	hypodermic	pachyderm
endemic	democracy	epidemic
geocentric	cyclist	motorcycle
synchronize	chronicle	chronometer
program	cyclone	geophysics
geode	chronic	chronology
anagram	recycle	demographic

graph (to write)	hydr (water)	log (to speak)
meter (measure)	micro (small)	phon (sound)

- -

graphite	barometer	telegraph
hydrant	symphony	dialogue
apologize	microchip	speedometer
microbe	ecology	telephone
diameter	photograph	kilometer
phonics	hydrate	microcosm
micrometer	millimeter	polygraph
autograph	logical	saxophone
hydra	hydraulic	hydroplane
analogy	seismograph	headphone

| photo (light) | phys (nature) | pol, polis (city) |
| scope (see, view) | sphere (ball) | tele (far, off) |

photocopier	bathysphere	hemisphere
telepathy	police	horoscope
policy	geophysics	stratosphere
biosphere	periscope	politician
telecast	Annapolis	physical
astrophysics	telegram	microscope
telethon	photocell	gyroscope
photogenic	metaphysics	telegraph
photometry	megalopolis	stethoscope
metropolis	physique	photography

aud (to hear)	bene, beni (well)	cap (the head)
ced, ceas, cess (to go, to yield)	cide (to cut, to kill)	clud, clos, clus (to shut)

benefit	germicide	auditorium
audio	auditory	foreclose
capital	capillary	recede
cease	beneficial	disclose
concise	incise	antecedent
audition	capitalize	preclude
benign	audit	secede
excise	beneficiary	captain
benefactor	pesticide	intercede
closet	seclude	capitol

cor, corp (body)	cred (to believe, trust)	dic, dict (to speak)
duce, duct (to lead)	equa, equi (even)	fac, fact, fect (to do)

- -

dedicate	equable	facsimile
corpse	deduction	equilibrium
faction	dictionary	manufacture
accredit	induct	credible
corporation	prediction	educate
discredit	conductor	predicate
diction	credentials	equivalent
abduct	corporal	credence
defect	factory	corpulent
equity	credit	equation

fer (to carry)	form (a shape)	grac, grat (pleasing, thankful)
grad, gress (to step)	hab, hib (to have, hold)	ject (to throw)

- -

deform	habit	inhabit
differ	gracious	congratulate
formal	inhibit	information
grace	regressing	gratify
transgress	infer	habituate
grateful	formula	objection
dejected	gratuity	conference
ferry	congress	inference
formation	habitat	degradable
centigrade	projectile	conjecture

lit (a letter)	loc, loq (to speak)	man (hand)
mem (mindful, remember)	miss, mit (to send)	mob, mot (to move)

motivate	missile	memoir
literacy	promote	literature
eloquent	literary	immobile
memento	memory	manacle
missionary	locomotion	emissary
mobile	colloquial	emancipate
memorable	maneuver	commission
manual	ventriloquist	literal
elocution	permission	memorial
manicure	manage	illiterate

numer (number)	ped (foot)	pens, pend (to hang)
port (to carry)	pos, pone (to put, place)	prim, princ (first)

export	primate	dispense
impostor	portable	innumerable
primary	position	pendulum
deportment	transport	millipede
appendix	principal	important
expedite	opposite	preposition
number	report	prince
centipede	impending	transpose
compensate	pedestrian	portfolio
numerous	pendant	numerator

quer, ques, quir (to ask)	scrib, script (to write)	sent, sens (to feel, perceive)
sist, stat (to stand)	spec, spect, spic (to see)	tain (to hold)

- -

maintain	circumspect	query
scribble	sentry	prescription
desist	scripture	consent
dissent	question	insistent
inscribe	consensus	auspicious
acquire	station	consistent
postscript	inspector	inquisition
require	entertain	description
sensation	spectator	specimen
request	abstain	pertain

tract (to pull)	val (be strong, worth)	ven, vent (to come)
vers, vert (to turn)	vid, vis (to see)	voc, vok (to call)

advertise	protract	extraction
convention	eventual	evaluate
attract	providence	introvert
evident	reverse	provoke
evoke	traction	televise
avocation	vocation	supervision
invisible	conversation	devaluate
convert	intervene	vocabulary
valiant	inverse	traverse
universe	validate	prevent

Appendix

Directions for a
Closed Word Sort

Materials
word sort cards
category cards or "key word" cards

Directions
1. Place the word sort category cards or the "key word" cards at the top of the table.
2. Place the word sort cards on the table.
3. Think about the categories as you look carefully at each word sort card and say the word slowly.
4. Place the word sort card under the category it matches.
5. Sort all of the word cards this way.
6. If there are words that do not fit into any of the categories, place them in an "out of sorts" category.
7. Have someone check your sort.

ir	ire	OUT OF SORTS
dirty	expire	liter
circus	retire	
firmly	fireproof	

Directions for an
Open Word Sort

Materials
word sort cards
blank category cards

Directions
1. Place the word sort cards on the table.
2. Look carefully at all of the cards and say the words slowly.
3. Think about how some of the words might be alike.
4. Place those cards together and write how the words are alike on a blank category card. Place the category card above the words that fit in that category. Sort the rest of the word cards this way.
5. If there are any word sort cards that do not fit into any of the categories, make an "out of sorts" category card and place those word sort cards under it.
6. Have someone check your work.

ends with en	*ends with on*	*out of sorts*
deafen	**carton**	**human**
children	**glutton**	**cousin**
spoken	**iron**	

Answer Keys:
Homophone Pairs With Long and Short Vowel Sounds (#1-#6)

#1

short a	short e	short i	short o	short u
rap	bread	him	knot	plum
wrap	bred	hymn	not	plumb
sac	cell	in		
sack	sell	inn		
tacks	cent	its		
tax	scent	it's		
	lead	knit		
	led	nit		
	read	tic		
	red	tick		

#2

short a	short e	short i	short o	short u	OUT OF SORTS
rap	bread	in	knot	plum	bare
wrap	bred	inn	not	plumb	bear
sac	cell	its			peak
sack	sell	it's			peek
tacks	cent	knit			
tax	scent	nit			
	lead	tic			
	led	tick			

#3

long a	long e	long i	long o	long u
made	dear	die	hole	blew
maid	deer	dye	whole	blue
main	meat	eye	oh	chute
Maine	meet	I	owe	shoot
	peace	hi	role	
	piece	high	roll	
	steal			
	steel			
	we'd			
	weed			

#4

long a	long e	long i	long o	long u	OUT OF SORTS
pail	creak	aisle	close	flu	cell
pale	creek	I'll	clothes	flue	sell
vain	feat	right	doe		in
vane	feet	write	dough		inn
	weak	sight	groan		
	week	site	grown		
			know		
			no		

#5

short vowel	long vowel
been	bail
bin	bale
cent	beat
sent	beet
in	cheap
inn	cheep
tacks	ewe
tax	you
which	hay
witch	hey
	loan
	lone
	real
	reel
	rose
	rows
	stake
	steak
	tail
	tale

#6

short vowel	long vowel	OUT OF SORTS
cent	flea	earn
sent	flee	furn
him	knead	foul
hymn	need	fowl
knot	plain	
not	plane	
rap	seam	
wrap	seem	
son	sew	
sun	so	
which	stile	
witch	style	
	way	
	weigh	

Answer Keys:

Homophones (#7–#8)

#7

homophones	not homophones
air-heir	base-bass
beech-beach	cake-cakes
break-brake	can-cannot
cell-sell	farm-harm
deer-dear	house-home
hey-hay	might-light
male-mail	name-names
passed-past	run-running
peace-piece	say-stay
pear-pair	shame-blame
plain-plane	wave-waved
prays-praise	
rain-rein	
red-read	
steak-stake	
tale-tail	
tax-tacks	
their-there	
way-weigh	

#8

homophones	not homophones
ant-aunt	be-see
ate-eight	can't-cannot
bale-bail	don't-did not
bear-bare	most-boast
cash-cache	need-needs
fair-fare	ran-fan
hair-hare	see-saw
jeans-genes	set-seat
main-mane	sled-sleigh
meet-meat	was-were
need-knead	
pale-pail	
peak-peek	
praise-preys	
rain-reign	
rap-wrap	
sail-sale	
seem-seam	
sleigh-slay	
they're-there	

Answer Keys:

Compound Words (#9–#10)

#9

compound words	not compound words
eyelid	coming
farmhouse	cushion
flashlight	dispenser
handmade	horse
headlight	isn't
landslide	magazine
nightmare	monkey
notebook	monster
outline	pitcher
skyscraper	snowy
snowstorm	sugar
thanksgiving	table
throughout	
toothache	
typewriter	
update	
upset	
windstorm	

#10

compound words	not compound words
basketball	bridge
coastline	coffee
cornhusk	counter
cornstarch	dictionary
courthouse	grounded
everybody	lighter
footbridge	mountainous
hairstyle	picture
headlight	plowed
newsstand	puppies
overflow	rainy
pancakes	senator
toothpaste	telephone
upright	waffle
waterproof	
windshield	

Answer Keys:

Compound Words (#11–#15)

#11

two-syllable compounds
barefoot
broadcast
chairman
downstream
footbridge
hillside
horseshoe
network
outside
paintbrush
sailboat
scarecrow
seasick
stagecoach
withdraw

three-syllable compounds
afternoon
anywhere
businessman
butterscotch
cheerleader
flowerpot
grandfather
overboard
policeman
summertime
thanksgiving
typewriter
underground
understand
waterproof

#12

two-syllable compounds
drugstore
grandson
hillside
paintbrush
proofread
rowboat
smallpox
spaceship
starfish
steamboat
teapot
weekend
withhold
within

three-syllable compounds
anything
buttermilk
candlestick
coffeepot
everyone
forever
grandchildren
however
mountainside
otherwise
quarterback
salesperson
townspeople
underline
undermine
waterproof

#13

two-syllable compounds
broomstick
cornstarch
football
headlight
hillside
notebook
pancakes
raindrops
sailboat
shoeshine
snowstorm
soapbox
stagecoach
toothpaste
within

three-syllable compounds
afternoon
anywhere
basketball
everyone
grandmother
however
masterpiece
peppermill
summertime
tablecloth
underground

OUT OF SORTS
pencil
pitcher
shepherd
slowly

#14

two-syllable compounds
flagpole
flashlight
football
highway
mainland
network
offspring
pancake
rooftop
scarecrow
starfish
wildlife
withhold
without

three-syllable compounds
anytime
buttermilk
everyone
forever
grandchildren
grandfather
masterpiece
overall
skyscraper
summertime
thanksgiving
typewriter
underline
understand
waterfall
whenever

#15

two-syllable compounds
baseball
bedroom
birthday
fireman
fireplace
flashlight
headlight
highway
indoor
outside
paintbrush
snowflake
stagecoach
textbook
warehouse
without

three-syllable compounds
afternoon
anything
astronaut
basketball
butterscotch
everyone
gingerbread
hamburger
however
overall
policeman
rattlesnake
waterproof
windowpane

Answer Keys:
Compound Words (#16)

#16

two-syllable compounds	three-syllable compounds	OUT OF SORTS
flashlight	everyone	playing
goldfish	fingerprint	propeller
peanut	flowerpot	refrigerator
proofread	mountainside	satisfaction
smallpox	overcast	
starfish	overlook	
steamboat	quarterback	
warehouse	rattlesnake	
weekend	salesperson	
wildlife	storekeeper	
without	summertime	
worthwhile	typewriter	
	waterway	
	whoever	

Answer Keys:
Contractions (#17–#19)

#17

contractions	not contractions
aren't	cannot
can't	had
doesn't	here
don't	his
he'll	into
here's	she
how's	should
isn't	that
I've	they
shouldn't	what
that's	where
they'll	would
they're	
we'd	
what's	
who's	
you'd	
you're	

#18

contractions	not contractions
aren't	does
doesn't	have
don't	hers
hadn't	that
hasn't	theirs
haven't	was
he'll	went
how's	within
I'm	your
let's	yours
that'll	
there's	
they'd	
they're	
wouldn't	
would've	
who'd	
who's	
you're	
you've	

#19

are family	not family	had/would family	will family
they're	aren't	he'd	he'll
we're	can't	I'd	I'll
you're	couldn't	she'd	it'll
	doesn't	there'd	she'll
	don't	they'd	that'll
	hadn't	we'd	they'll
	hasn't	who'd	we'll
	haven't	you'd	you'll
	isn't		
	shouldn't		
	wasn't		
	weren't		

Answer Keys:
Contractions (#20-#22)

#20

is/has family		have family	us family	will family
he's	who's	I've	let's	he'll
here's	why's	could've		I'll
how's		should've		it'll
it's		they've	am family	she'll
she's		we've	I'm	that'll
that's		would've		there'll
there's		you've		they'll
what's				we'll
when's				you'll
where's				

#21

am family	are family	had/would family	have family	is/has family	not family	us family	will family
I'm	they're	he'd	I've	here's	can't	let's	he'll
	we're	there'd	they've	how's	doesn't		I'll
		they'd	you've	what's	don't		it'll
		we'd		who's	hasn't		she'll
		who'd			haven't		that'll
					isn't		
					wasn't		
					weren't		
					wouldn't		

#22

am family	are family	had/would family	have family	is/has family	not family	us family	will family
I'm	they're	he'd	could've	he's	don't	let's	I'll
	you're	she'd	they've	here's	hadn't		it'll
		you'd	would've	how's	hasn't		
				she's	isn't		**OUT OF SORT**
				what's	wasn't		cannot
				where's	weren't		could
				who's	wouldn't		shell
							went

Answer Keys:
Contractions and Compound Words (#23-#25)

#23

contractions	compound words
aren't	baseball
can't	bedroom
couldn't	cannot
could've	cornhusk
he'll	flagpole
here's	handprint
he's	lighthouse
isn't	mailbox
it's	newscast
she'd	stairway
shouldn't	sunlight
that'll	without
that's	
they're	
they've	
we'll	
where's	
you'll	

#24

contractions	compound words
couldn't	airplane
could've	birdbath
hasn't	daylight
he's	football
it's	hairbrush
I've	herself
she'll	landmark
should've	lifeguard
they'd	lifetime
they're	outdoors
we'd	popcorn
weren't	raindrop
we're	seafood
where's	toothpaste
you'll	
you're	

#25

contractions	Compound Words
can't	cannot
don't	cupboard
I'm	cupcake
isn't	hillside
let's	houseboat
she'd	otherwise
she'll	runway
shouldn't	sailboat
that'll	teapot
there's	wherever
they'll	windpipe
we'll	
weren't	**OUT OF SORTS**
would've	boat
you'll	business
	happy
	house

180

Answer Keys:

Doubling the Final Consonant When Adding *ed* and *ing* (CVC Pattern) (#26-#27)

#26

double the final consonant	don't double the final consonant
beg	cheer
can	chew
dip	eat
drop	farm
fan	fish
hop	fool
hug	hunt
knit	keep
net	mark
pad	need
pet	rain
rub	roar
stop	push
tip	spill
trip	
win	

#27

double the final consonant	don't double the final consonant
chop	ask
drag	blend
drop	call
jog	fill
knot	fool
net	hiss
pat	jump
pin	learn
rob	melt
scar	munch
ship	quit
slip	seal
snap	twist
step	wreck
thin	
tip	

Answer Keys:

Dropping the Final *e* When Adding *ed* and *ing* (#28-#29)

#28

drop the final *e*	don't drop the final *e*
bake	clean
dare	comb
file	cross
flame	farm
grade	gain
ice	heal
like	lift
name	loan
note	miss
pipe	point
place	pull
ride	push
save	smell
shade	stamp
smile	
store	

#29

drop the final *e*	don't drop the final *e*
chase	help
chime	march
flame	pad
grade	plan
make	point
mine	rob
note	shop
owe	speed
pile	stamp
pipe	star
price	thin
race	want
ride	
save	
shape	
strive	
trade	
tune	

Answer Keys:

Doubling the Final Consonant and Dropping the final *e* When Adding Endings (#30–#34)

#30

double the final consonant	drop the final *e*
chop	blame
fan	care
hop	chase
knot	dare
trip	file
mop	hope
pad	like
pet	line
pin	score
rob	shake
scar	smile
slip	store
snap	take
sob	tame
trap	use

#31

double the final consonant	drop the final *e*
bat	blame
drag	chime
fan	file
jog	fume
knit	hope
mop	ice
net	like
pin	line
plug	mine
slip	note
ship	race
sob	save
star	score
thin	skate
trap	trade

#32

double the final consonant	drop the final *e*	OUT OF SORTS
drop	bake	mark
grab	care	nest
jog	dare	scoop
knot	grade	shout
ship	hope	
slip	line	
step	price	
trap	race	
tug	save	
wag	shade	
	shake	
	slope	
	smile	
	stare	
	tame	
	wave	

#33

double the final consonant	drop the final *e*	no change
drip	grade	blind
drop	hide	bump
hop	hope	heal
rip	make	hunt
sag	move	moan
shut	smile	pelt
sip	snake	seat
slap	stripe	shout
stop	vote	slant
wed		smell
		snack

#34

double the final consonant	drop the final *e*	no change
clap	double	bead
dot	glide	duck
fan	name	fool
grip	slope	heat
pin	tape	hint
plan	tune	hook
ship	wave	melt
shop	vote	milk
step		miss
tap		scold
		sift
		slump

Answer Keys:

CVC, CVCC, CVVC and VCCV Syllable Structures (#35-#37)

#35		#36		#37	
CVC pattern with short vowels	CVCC pattern with short vowels	CVC pattern with short vowels	CVVC pattern with long vowels	VCCV no doubed consonant	VCCV doubed consonant
clip	cash	can	cheek	elbow	blossom
drag	jump	fit	cheer	fabric	button
fan	kiss	hug	claim	helmet	coffee
fin	lift	hop	fail	husband	comment
fix	lock	lip	gain	orbit	copper
hit	melt	net	groan	pardon	funny
hop	milk	pad	heat	person	gallows
jog	miss	pet	jeep	pencil	letter
pan	pick	pop	loan	picnic	passage
pen	pill	rub	need	plastic	slipper
pit	send	step	roar	reptile	soccer
rob	task	tap	seam	winter	spelling
run	wink	tug	seal		sudden
stop			speak		traffic
ten			trail		village
then			wait		wedding
wet			weep		worry
					yellow

Answer Keys:

Stressed First and Second Syllable Words (#38-#39)

#38		#39	
stressed first syllable	stressed second syllable	stressed first syllable	stressed second syllable
atom	although	album	beside
camel	beyond	cactus	cement
comic	cartoon	carpet	complete
dessert	deny	children	debate
dozen	elect	chili	decide
figure	forget	comfort	enjoy
habit	hotel	habit	event
lily	police	market	obey
navy	prepare	midget	polite
panic	pretend	morning	pollute
pony	propel	orbit	prevent
prison	raccoon	pilgrim	remain
siren	repair	puddle	reveal
spinach	select	seldom	severe
super	unite	temper	
		walrus	

Answer Keys:

Abstract Vowel Sounds of "a" (#40–#42)

#40

al	au	aw
bald	cause	crawl
call	fraud	dawn
chalk	gauze	draw
false	haunch	drawn
mall	launch	fawn
malt	sauce	gnaw
salt	taught	lawn
scald	vault	pawn
walk		shawl
waltz		straw
		thaw
		yawn

#41

al	al	al
balk	caught	bawl
ball	cause	claw
chalk	fraud	crawl
false	hauled	drawn
halt	haunch	gnaw
salt	haunt	hawk
scald	launch	jaw
small	sauce	raw
stalk		shawl
stall		slaw
waltz		sprawl

#42

al	au	aw	OUT OF SORTS
bald	cause	bawl	clown
called	fraud	caw	frown
false	haunt	crawl	full
halt	sauce	draw	melt
malt	taught	drawl	
scald		fawn	
small		lawn	
stall		raw	
wall		sprawl	
		squawk	
		thaw	
		yawn	

Answer Keys:

Adding Plural Endings (#43–#45)

#43

add s	add es
adult	arch
apple	beach
bath	boss
braid	box
cow	brush
exam	dish
label	gas
nurse	guess
puzzle	inch
siren	index
square	latch
street	leash
string	lunch
tulip	six
	tax
	witch

#44

add s	add es
horn	ash
horse	atlas
judge	batch
parent	bonus
pebbles	bunch
result	bush
riddle	class
rule	crash
shadow	cross
sleeve	dish
	flash
	finch
	fox
	index
	latch
	loss
	pass
	peach
	rich
	tax

#45

add s	add es	OUT OF SORTS
actor	ash	deer
adult	bonus	geese
base	box	oxen
coin	brush	sheep
exam	bunch	woman
mitten	bush	
ruler	class	
spice	fish	
wire	inch	
	kiss	
	latch	
	lynx	
	pass	
	peach	
	push	
	rich	

Answer Keys:
Adding Plural Endings (#46-#49)

#46

add *s*	add *es*	change *y* to *i* and add *es*
badge	arch	army
chair	atlas	berry
robot	batch	bully
seat	class	city
wagon	dish	country
	gas	daisy
	guess	jelly
	inch	party
	leash	pony
	lunch	sky
	mass	
	notch	
	push	
	six	
	tax	

#47

add *s*	add *es*	change *y* to *i* and add *es*
acorn	arch	baby
cabin	ax	body
dragon	beach	bunny
string	crash	copy
teacher	cross	jury
train	fox	lady
	gas	lily
	glass	penny
	hitch	
	inch	
	index	
	iris	
	leash	
	pass	
	toss	
	watch	

#48

add *s*	add *es*	change *y* to *i* and add *es*
bump	dress	county
hill	mix	cry
chick	lunch	daisy
medal	bus	ruby
park	push	trophy
crayon	crash	
bath	fox	
cousin	hitch	**OUT OF SORTS**
	pass	calf
	match	elf
	atlas	man
	bench	sheep
	glass	

#49

add *s*	add *es*	change *y* to *i* and add *es*
path	dress	buggy
sneeze	brush	country
trouser	inch	fly
ruler	bunch	lady
	bus	pastry
	ax	posy
	mix	spy
	class	
	notch	**OUT OF SORTS**
	hitch	deer
	kiss	man
	fish	sheep
	index	woman
	bush	
	rich	

Answer Keys:
Open and Closed Syllable Structures with Short and Long Vowel Sounds (#50-#53)

#50

open syllable	closed syllable
label	atom
music	camel
pony	civil
ripen	closet
robot	credit
shiny	comic
siren	decade
sofa	digit
solar	dozen
spicy	figure
spoken	habit
unit	honey
	honor
	jacket
	lemon
	never
	novel
	timid

#51

open syllable	closed syllable
music	comic
navy	credit
pilot	edit
pony	figure
pupil	frigid
radar	govern
ripen	honey
ruby	lemon
soda	lever
solo	lizard
spoken	menu
tulip	solid
unit	spinach
zebra	timid
	travel
	vanish

#52

open syllable	closed syllable
china	closet
crater	comet
cocoa	decade
evil	driven
female	finish
flavor	frigid
item	habit
major	image
pirate	legend
profile	level
program	money
siren	novel
solar	olive
spicy	
super	
vacant	
widen	

#53

open syllable	closed syllable	OUT OF SORTS
baby	atom	grand
bacon	camel	moods
fever	chili	speed
final	civil	troll
frequent	clever	
future	finish	
glider	gravel	
pupil	honest	
photo	legend	
ripen	olive	
robot	profit	
rumor	taxi	
super		
tuna		

Answer Keys:

Open and Closed Syllable Structures with Short and Long Vowel Sounds (#54-#55)

#54

open syllable with the VCV pattern	closed syllable with the VCCV pattern
before	admit
decide	cartoon
label	confess
paper	confuse
pirate	dentist
pony	discuss
radar	enjoy
robot	enter
ruby	excite
spicy	forbid
student	ignore
super	indeed
tulip	observe
vacant	perform
widen	until

#55

open syllable with the VCV pattern	closed syllable with the VCCV pattern
able	album
baby	basket
basic	center
cozy	chimney
even	compass
famous	contest
favor	custom
female	dolphin
final	elbow
Friday	engine
lazy	enter
legal	expert
	fabric
	furnish
	garden
	helmet
	husband
	index

Answer Keys:

Long Vowel Patterns in the Stressed Syllable (#56-#57)

#56

aCe words	ai words	ay words	open syllable long a words
baseball	contain	dismay	cradle
behave	dainty	grayish	lazy
embrace	drainage	maybe	nation
engrave	exclaim	prayer	rabies
graceful	painter	sayings	sacred
parade	raining	today	shaky
safety	raisin		skater
	refrain		vapor
	sailor		

#57

aCe words	ai words	ay words	open syllable long a words
behave	await	astray	basil
engrave	draining	betray	crater
erase	exclaim	crayfish	nation
estate	failure	daydream	rabies
graceful	mailboxes	daylight	savor
skateboard	railroad	decay	wafer
statement	remain	maybe	
	tailor	payment	
		player	

Answer Keys:

Long Vowel Patterns in the Stressed Syllable (#58-#63)

#58

aCe words	ai words	ay words	open syllable long a words
bracelet	campaign	astray	data
cascade	explain	crayon	fable
create	mainland	decay	fatal
grapefruit	painful	hooray	ladle
mistake	rainbow	layer	nation
parade	raincoat	today	raven
pavement	strainer		savor
	sustain		shaky
	traitor		

#59

aCe words	ai words	ay words	open syllable long a words	OUT OF SORTS
basement	complain	astray	April	lead
escape	mailman	decay	glacier	motor
graceful	rainy	graying	hatred	seeing
grapevines	refrain	maybe	navy	while
lakeside	tailor	playful	patient	
pavement	waiter	today	shaky	
scrape				
snakebite				

#60

ee words	ea words	ie words
agree	beaver	achieve
breezy	conceal	apiece
canteen	defeat	believe
cheetah	eager	besiege
degree	easel	diesel
freeway	easy	relief
greeting	ideal	relieve
indeed	mislead	retrieve
kneecap	release	
sleeping	repeal	
tureen	weasel	

#61

ee words	ea words	ie words
baleen	appeal	achieve
between	disease	belief
breeze	eager	besiege
degree	increase	brief
freeway	meanwhile	diesel
greenish	mislead	relief
greeting	ordeal	relieve
indeed	peanut	retrieve
redeem	release	
steeple	reveal	
steeply		
sweeping		

#62

ee words	ea words	ie words	OUT OF SORTS
gleeful	ideal	achieve	gated
between	defeat	relieve	training
esteem	eager	relief	blown
tweezers	reveal	believe	music
unseen	ordeal	besiege	
kneecap	mislead	apiece	
freedom	disease		
between	cheaply		
proceed	peanut		
sweeping	meanwhile		

#63

open syllable long e words	eCe long e words	ei long e words
cedar	compete	caffeine
depot	delete	ceiling
even	deplete	either
fever	discrete	leisure
legal	extreme	neither
meter	precede	perceive
prefix	recede	receipt
recent	serene	receive
sequence	supreme	seizure
species		
tepees		
zebra		

Answer Keys:

Long Vowel Patterns in the Stressed Syllable (#64–#67)

#64

open syllable long e words	eCe long e words	ei long e words
decent	complete	caffeine
detour	concede	ceiling
female	convene	conceive
fever	delete	deceive
legal	discrete	either
meter	impede	leisure
preview	replete	neither
recent	secede	receipt
regal	serene	receive
species	stampede	
veto		

#65

open syllable long e words	eCe long e words	ei long e words	OUT OF SORTS
detour	complete	caffeine	choose
female	convene	ceiling	smart
fever	deplete	either	smell
legal	recede	leisure	tuned
prefix	supreme	neither	
regal	trapeze	perceive	
		receipt	
		receive	
		seizure	

#66

iCe words	igh words	iCC words	y long i words	open syllable long i words
advise	fighter	binder	defy	biker
dislike	highway	childish	dryer	diner
divide	lighten	climber	flyer	dining
iceberg	sightsee	remind	July	pirate
invite	tighten	rewind	typist	spider
sidewalk	tonight	wildcat		title
				visor

#67

iCe words	igh words	iCC words	y long i words	open syllable long i words
decide	delight	binder	bypass	bridle
driveway	flighty	blindfold	dryer	icy
finely	highness	climber	hydrant	rhino
nightmare	highway	findings	nylon	rival
surprise	mighty	resign	sinus	writer
widely	nighttime	sinus	tyrant	
		unkind		
		wildlife		

Answer Keys:

Long Vowel Patterns in the Stressed Syllable (#68-#72)

#68

iCe words	igh words	iCC words	y long i words	open syllable long i words
confide	highway	assign	apply	bison
delight	lighthouse	bindings	gyro	cider
excite	lightning	design	rely	imply
iceberg	pliers	kindness	rhyming	item
ninety	sightsee	remind	stylish	miser
recline	tonight	spyglass		
survive	unkind			

#69

iCe words	igh words	iCC words	y long i words	open syllable long i	OUT OF SORTS
despite	delight	assign	gyro	dining	dining
ignite	highway	climber	hybrid	diver	even
invite	mighty	findings	python	item	leave
oblige	sightless	remind	rhyme	minus	trapped
provide		rewind		slimy	waiting
refine				timer	
				tripod	

#70

oCe words	oa words	oCC words	ow words	open syllabe long o words
arose	coastal	goldfinch	crowbar	cobra
enclose	goalie	polka	glowworm	donate
explode	roadway	poster	rowers	motor
homework	unload	revolt	snowflake	notice
lonely		soldier	snowshoe	ocean
lonesome		stroller		pony
		tollbooth		protein
				soda

#71

oCe words	oa words	oCC words	ow words	open syllabe long o words
coleslaw	boathouse	almost	disown	frozen
dispose	coaching	coldness	lower	local
erode	coastal	enroll	snowshoe	moment
foretold	coattail	molding		odor
hopeful	goalie	revolt		potion
	roadside	withhold		rodent
	soapy			rotate
	toadstool			sofa

#72

oCe words	oa words	oCC words	ow words	open syllabe long o words
awoke	approach	almost	aglow	cobra
erode	coastal	coldness	bestow	hostess
explode	coaster	enroll	disown	locate
homeless	goalie	moldings	snowfall	moment
hopeful	loafer	postcard	snowshoe	nomad
	roadway	uphold		notion
				program
				social

Answer Keys:
Long Vowel Patterns in the Stressed Syllable (#73-#77)

#73

oCe words	oa words	oCC words	ow words	open syllabe long o words	OUT OF SORTS
notebook	afloat	molten	owner	pronoun	plot
smoky	approach	postage	snowball	motor	boots
awake	floating	smolder	goldfinch	grocer	pinned
rosebush	toaster	behold	bowling	hotel	hotter
homesick		almost	aglow	donate	
explode			disown		

#74

uCe words	open syllable long u words
amuse	bugle
conclude	futile
confuse	future
consume	human
dilute	humid
exclude	humor
excuse	pupil
include	rumor
jukebox	student
lukewarm	super
misuse	truly
pollute	tumor
reduce	tuna
resume	tunic
ruling	tutor

#75

uCe words	open syllable long u words
abuse	bugle
amuse	futile
compute	future
conclude	human
confuse	humid
exclude	music
include	sumac
lukewarm	ruby
perfume	rumor
protrude	student
reduce	super
ruling	truly
salute	tuba
tubeless	tulip
	tumor
	tuna

#76

uCe words	open syllable long u words
abuse	bugle
acute	futile
compute	future
confuse	humid
dilute	humor
dispute	music
exclude	pupil
excuse	ruby
include	rumor
lukewarm	student
resume	sumac
ruling	tulip
salute	truly
yuletide	tumor
	tuna
	tutor

#77

uCe words	open syllable long u words
dispute	humid
excuse	music
include	pupil
lukewarm	rumor
misuse	ruby
preclude	super
presume	suture
protrude	tuba
reduce	tulip
resume	truly
ruling	tunic
salute	tutor
useful	
yuletide	

	OUT OF SORTS
	center
	dungeon
	planning
	ugly

Answer Keys:

Short and Long Vowel Patterns in the Stressed Syllable (#78–#83)

#78

short a words	aCe words	ai words	ay words	open syllable long a words
cannon	behave	await	grayish	basis
gallop	debate	complain	mayor	lazy
hammer	disgrace	failure	portray	nation
lantern	engrave	mainland	prayer	radar
massive	erase	railroad	today	
satin	estate	raincoat		
scatter	persuade	sailor		

#79

short a words	aCe words	ai words	ay words	open syllable long a words
ambush	bracelet	drainage	crayon	agent
canvas	crater	failure	maybe	basic
daddy	create	mailbox	okay	fable
expand	debate	painter	payment	lazy
flashlight	engage	rainbow	portray	
	parade	trainer	sayings	
	persuade			
	safety			
	skateboard			

#80

short a words	aCe words	ai words	ay words	open syllable long a words	OUT OF SORTS
banter	amaze	acquaint	betray	lazy	cartoon
cattle	bracelet	rainbow	daydream	nation	shook
expand	baseball	strainer	layer	rabies	smiling
patent	basement	tailor	maybe	radar	speeder
ranch	mistake		okay		
	safety		playmate		
	skater				

#81

short e	short ea	long ee	long ea	long ie	open syllable long e	long eCe	long ei
connects	deafen	agree	appeal	achieve	being	compete	ceiling
exit	heavy	degree	cheaply	believe	cedar	serene	either
	leather	redeem	eager	belief	event	trapeze	receipt
	ready	succeed	ordeal	relief	prefix		receive
			peanut				

#82

short e	short ea	long ee	long ea	long ie	open syllable long e	long eCe	long ei
beggar	dreadful	asleep	creature	relief	female	delete	neither
connect	feather	cheetah	defeat	relieve	legal	impede	perceive
distress	healthy	freedom	ideal	retrieve	species	stampede	seizure
	heavy	greeting	release				
	steady	sweeten	reveal				

#83

short e	short ea	long ee	long ea	long ie	open syllable long e	long eCe	long ei	OUT OF SORTS
attend	heavy	between	beaver	achieve	decent	convene	caffeine	acorn
confess	pheasant	greenish	creature	apiece	elect	precede	leisure	pinned
effect	ready	seedling	eager	debrief	meter	supreme	receive	plated
	treasure	tureen						snoring

Answer Keys:
Short and Long Vowel Patterns in the Stressed Syllable (#84-#89)

#84

short i	y short i	iCe long i	igh long i	iCC long i	y long i	open syllable
insect	rhythm	decline	fighter	behind	apply	cider
opinion	gypsy	divide	mighty	blindfold	gyro	iris
simmer	physics	invite	nightmare	remind	hydrant	pirate
		lively	sightsee	unkind	July	rival
		precise		wildcat	python	sinus

#85

short i	y Short i	iCe long i	igh long i	iCC long i	y long i	open syllable
dinner	gypsy	arrive	highway	assign	cyclist	minus
illness	physics	despite	lighten	bindings	dryer	rifle
insect	symbol	ignite	sightsee	findings	flyer	slimy
pillow		invite		wildcat	pliers	tripod
sizzle		ninety			rely	
					supply	

#86

short i	y short i	iCe long i	igh long i	iCC long i	y long i	open syllable	OUT OF SORTS
enlist	cymbal	dining	delight	childhood	defy	pirate	cartoon
index	gypsy	icy	lightning	climber	flyer	rival	needless
ribbon	rhythm	invite	sightless	wildcat	flying	title	purple
	system		sightsee		imply	visor	street
					nylon		

#87

short o	oCe words	oa words	oCC words	ow words	open syllable
cobwebs	explode	afloat	polka	crowbar	local
copper	homework	floating	poster	lower	notice
chopstick	notebook	roadway	soldier	rowers	pony
honest	propose	soapy	uphold	snowstorm	soda
novel		toaster			total
profit		unload			trophy

#88

short o	oCe words	oa words	oCC words	ow words	open syllable
forgot	awoke	boater	enroll	below	frozen
lobby	decode	coastline	poster	owner	moment
modern	homesick	goalie	postman	rowing	odor
pocket	lonesome	loafer	tollbooth	showdown	social
rotten	stovepipe	roadway		snowman	sofa
		toadstool			

#89

short o	oCe words	oa words	oCC words	ow words	open syllable	OUT OF SORTS
bottle	erode	boathouse	folktales	reblown	locate	battle
chopstick	hopeful	coattail	postage	rowing	notion	driver
forgot	lonely	soapy	poster	snowball	spoken	painting
problem	lonesome	unload	toaster	snowfall	total	splatter
respond						
robber						

Answer Keys:
Short and Long Vowel Patterns in the Stressed Syllable (#90-#92)

#90

short u words	uCe words	open syllable words
cluster	compute	future
erupt	confuse	human
fumble	dilute	humid
funny	dispute	music
grumpy	excuse	pupil
hundred	jukebox	rumor
husband	presume	truly
jungle	reduce	tulip
publish	salute	tuna
punish		tunic
rugged		

#91

short u words	uCe words	open syllable words
clumsy	abuse	bugle
fumble	acute	humor
instruct	conclude	music
mustang	dilute	rumor
mustard	excuse	student
publish	include	sumac
pumpkin	jukebox	truly
rustle	perfume	tumor
snuggle	resume	tuna
thunder	yuletide	tutor

#92

short u words	uCe words	open syllable words	OUT OF SORTS
chuckle	amuse	bugle	apple
custom	exclude	futile	moved
disgust	excuse	human	thousand
distrust	misuse	humor	trained
erupt	pollute	pupil	
fumble	reduce	rumor	
hundred	ruling	student	
instruct		super	
public		tumor	
rugged			

Answer Keys:
R-Controlled Vowel Patterns in the Stressed Syllable (#93-#95)

#93

ar (marker)	are	air	ar (narrate)
cartwheel	barefoot	aircraft	carriage
charter	barely	airport	marrow
garnet	compare	airwaves	narrow
marble	declare	dairy	parent
parka	prepare	hairpin	sparrow
parkway	rarest	prairie	tariff
parsley	spareribs	repair	vary
party			
tardy			

#94

ar (marker)	are	air	ar (narrate)
apart	aware	aircraft	barren
darkness	beware	airlines	carol
farmhouse	carefree	airmail	carrot
garland	careful	despair	marriage
garlic	declare	fairground	narrate
harvest	prepare	fairway	parent
larva	warehouse	haircut	tariff
marshal			
sarcasm			

#95

ar (marker)	are	air	ar (narrate)	OUT OF SORTS
barber	bareback	affair	barracks	alive
cartridge	compare	chairman	barrel	initial
farther	declare	dairy	marrow	meeting
margin	prepare	repair	narrate	opinion
parcel	rarely	staircase	parish	
partner	spareribs	stairway	parrot	
starchy			scarab	

194

Answer Keys:
R-Controlled Vowel Patterns in the Stressed Syllable (#96–#101)

#96

er	ear (heard)	ear (fear)	eer	ere
berry	early	appear	career	adhere
derrick	earthen	dearest	deerskin	merely
herdsman	relearn	dreary	sheerest	peering
jersey	searchlight	fearful	veneer	revere
nervous	unearned	gearshift		severe
perfect	yearning			sincere
person				
prefer				
verbal				

#97

er	ear (heard)	ear (fear)	eer	ere
gerbil	early	appear	cheerful	austere
herbal	earthquake	clearing	deerskin	cashmere
mermaid	learner	dearest	leery	hereby
merry	rehearse	teardrop	peering	merely
perky	relearn		steerage	severe
reverse	research			
sermon	unearned			
thermos	yearning			

#98

er	ear (heard)	ear (fear)	eer	ere	OUT OF SORTS
hermit	earthworm	bearded	deerskin	adhere	jumping
kerchief	learner	clearing	jeering	hereby	nonsense
perfect	pearly	dearest	leery	revere	penpal
reserve	research	fearful	sheerest	sincere	witness
	unearned	nearby			
	yearning	spearhead			
		tearful			
		yearbook			

#99

ir words	ire words
birdhouse	afire
birthday	attire
circle	desire
circus	expire
confirm	firefly
dirty	firehouse
firmly	fireproof
girlfriend	inquire
irksome	perspire
shirttail	rehire
sirloin	require
skirmish	retire
twirler	tiredness
whirlpool	tiresome
whirlwind	wiretap

#100

ir words	ire words
astir	acquire
birthmark	admire
chirping	attire
circle	desire
circuit	entire
dirty	expire
firmly	fireman
flirting	fireplace
girlfriend	fireproof
irksome	inquire
sirloin	inspire
swirling	perspire
thirsty	rehire
twirler	retire
whirlpool	tiresome

#101

ir words	ire words	OUT OF SORTS
admire	aspire	answer
affirm	direful	liter
birdbath	entire	physical
birdseed	expire	sitting
birthstone	fireman	
chirping	fireproof	
circuit	inquire	
confirm	inspire	
directions	perspire	
firmly	rehire	
flirting	retire	
irksome	tiresome	
virtue		
whirlpool		

195

Answer Keys:

R-Controlled Vowel Patterns in the Stressed Syllable (#102-#107)

#102

or words	ore words	oar words	our words
cornstarch	adore	aboard	courthouse
floral	before	boarding	courtyard
forfeit	explore	boardwalk	fourteen
fortress	ignore	coarsely	mournful
forty	restore	hoarding	sources
horseback	shoreline	hoarsely	yourself
shortcake	storeroom		
snorkel			
story			
torchlight			
torrent			

#103

or words	ore words	oar words	our words
border	adore	aboard	courtyard
corking	boredom	boarding	foursome
corner	galore	boardwalk	fourteen
cornmeal	restore	coarsely	pouring
cornstarch	shoreline	coarseness	sources
forceful	storefront	hoarseness	
forfeit			
forging			
porridge			
shortage			
sportsman			
torment			
tortoise			

#104

or words	ore words	oar words	our words	OUT OF SORTS
corncob	ashore	aboard	courtroom	bookroom
porpoise	before	boardroom	courtship	fierceness
porthole	deplore	coarsely	fourteen	shook
portrait	ignore	coarseness	mournful	sorrow
shortcake	restore	hoarseness	pouring	
snorkel	scoreless			
stormy	shorebird			
torchlight	storeroom			

#105

ur words	ure words
burglar	assure
bursting	brochure
curbstone	endure
curfew	ensure
cursor	impure
curtain	mature
flurry	obscure
furnace	obscure
further	procure
plural	purebred
surgeon	secure
turban	surefire
turkey	surely
turnip	unsure
turnstile	
turtle	

#106

ur words	ure words
burden	assure
burly	brochure
currant	endure
curry	impure
cursive	mature
curtain	pressure
curvy	procure
furnish	purebred
furrow	secure
hurdle	surefire
jury	surely
surgeon	unsure
surplus	
surrey	
Thursday	
turnip	
turquoise	
turret	

#107

ur words	ure words	OUT OF SORTS
burden	assure	flute
burglar	brochure	insane
curfew	endure	jersey
curtain	ensure	shaken
during	impure	
furrow	mature	
gurgle	obscure	
hurdle	secure	
hurry	surefire	
juror	unsure	
murder		
purple		
rural		
surplus		
turret		
turtle		

Answer Keys:
Abstract Vowel Combinations in the Stressed Syllable (#108-#113)

#108

oo (food)	ew	oo (foot)
aloof	anew	cookbook
bassoon	cashew	cookout
cartoon	chewy	footage
harpoon	dewdrop	football
lagoon	pewter	foothills
maroon	renew	footprints
moody	skewer	rookie
noodle	steward	sooty
poodle		woodland
raccoon		woodpile
shampoo		
toothache		

#109

oo (food)	ew	oo (foot)
aloof	askew	bookshelf
baboon	cashew	bookworm
balloon	chewy	cookbook
bassoon	crewman	cookout
cartoon	dewdrop	footage
cocoon	jewel	footprints
doodle	pewter	mistook
kazoo	skewer	rookie
monsoon		woodchuck
noodle		woodland
rooster		woodwind

#110

oy words	oi words	ou words	ow words
boycott	avoid	counsel	allow
destroy	doily	counter	blower
employ	exploit	county	coward
enjoy	poison	devour	cowhand
oyster	rejoice	doubtful	drowsy
royal		foundry	endow
soybean		mountain	rowdy
voyage		mousetrap	towel
		profound	

#111

oy words	oi words	ou words	ow words
ahoy	doily	bounty	chowder
boycott	exploit	council	downfall
employ	loiter	counsel	dowry
joyful	moisture	devour	drowsy
loyal	poison	fountain	prowler
oyster	rejoice	mountain	shower
royal		mouthwash	tower
voyage		scoundrel	vowel

#112

oo (food)	ew	oo (foot)	oy	oi	ou	ow
cartoon	anew	bookcase	annoy	appoint	doubtful	brownie
harpoon	crewman	footage	destroy	exploit	fountain	chowder
moody	jewel	football	enjoy	moisture	profound	drowsy
	pewter	raccoon	loyal	poison		powder
	skewer	woodwind		rejoice		rowdy

#113

oo (food)	ew	oo (foot)	oy	oi	ou	ow
lagoon	anew	bookcase	boycott	appoint	bounty	flower
moody	askew	cookbook	employ	moisture	foundry	tower
noodle	chewy	footprints	enjoy		mouthwash	trowel
shampoo	dewdrop	mistook	joyful		profound	
toothache	jewel	rookie	loyal			
			voyage			

197

Answer Keys:
Abstract Vowel Combinations in the Unstressed Syllable (#114-#117)

#114

ain words	*an* words	*en* words	*in* words	*on* words
bargain	airman	aspen	basin	apron
captain	organ	barren	penguin	button
certain	tartan	darken	resin	caldron
curtain	turban	garden	urchin	falcon
villain	urban	given		prison
	yeoman	mitten		treason
		swollen		wagon
		warden		

#115

ain words	*an* words	*en* words	*in* words	*on* words
bargain	human	chicken	cousin	bacon
certain	organ	children	goblin	bison
chaplain	orphan	deafen	muffin	carton
chieftain	seaman	kitten	muslin	glutton
fountain	sultan	siren		iron
mountain	yeoman	spoken		
villain		strengthen		
		thicken		

#116

al words	*il* words	*ile* words	*el* words	*le* words
global	April	fragile	bagel	beagle
medal	evil	futile	hazel	bottle
neutral	fossil	hostile	model	bubble
normal	nostril	missile	parcel	needle
pedal	stencil	sterile	towel	pickle
plural			weasel	purple
spiral				twinkle

#117

al words	*il* words	*ile* words	*el* words	*le* words
central	lentil	fragile	bushel	beetle
crystal	nostril	missile	diesel	bridle
loyal	pencil		flannel	cackle
mammal	tonsil		panel	cuddle
normal	tranquil		squirrel	docile
petal				eagle
plural				middle
signal				mumble
				struggle
				wrinkle

Answer Keys:

Abstract Vowel Combinations in the Unstressed Syllable (#118–#119)

#118

ar words	*er* words	*or* words
altar	banner	armor
burglar	consumer	director
cheddar	cylinder	doctor
cougar	fender	editor
dollar	founder	favor
grammar	lever	governor
hangar	scooter	mirror
molar	skater	splendor
peculiar	tweezers	tremor
pillar		vapor
sugar		

#119

ar words	*er* words	*or* words
briar	beginner	emperor
burglar	blister	equator
cellar	cheaper	meteor
circular	coaster	surveyor
cougar	dreamer	traitor
lunar	fiercer	vendor
molar	founder	visitor
nectar	jogger	
polar	ledger	
singular	planner	
	reader	
	shopper	
	trooper	

Answer Keys:

Common Prefixes (#120–#121)

#120

dis words	*en* words	*fore* words	*in* words
discharge	enable	forearm	inboard
disclose	enact	forehand	income
disfigure	encode	forehead	indent
dishonest	enforce	foremost	infield
disinfect	engulf	foresee	inflame
disorder	enjoin	foreshadow	inland
disregard	enlist	foresight	inseam
distrust			insight

#121

dis words	*en* words	*fore* words	*in* words
disable	enable	forehead	inboard
disarm	encase	foremost	income
disfavor	endear	forerunner	inlaid
dishonest	enfold	foresight	inmate
disinfect	engulf	foresight	input
disloyal	enjoy		inset
disorder	enlist		
disregard	enroll		
	enslave		
	entomb		

Answer Keys:

Common Prefixes (#122-#125)

#122

dis **words**	*en* **words**	*fore* **words**	*in* **words**	OUT OF SORTS
disappear	endear	foreclose	income	misplace
disclose	engulf	foreleg	indoors	preview
discomfort	enlarge	foreman	inland	reject
discover	enrage	foremost	input	unjust
disfavor	enrich	foresight	inside	
dislike	ensnare	forethought	insight	
disobey	entrust			

#123

mis **words**	*pre* **words**	*re* **words**	*un* **words**
miscount	predate	readjust	unafraid
misgivings	predawn	reclaim	unequal
mismanage	preexisting	recycle	uneven
mismatch	premature	reelect	unfair
misplace	preschool	refill	unfreeze
mistrust	pretest	relearn	unleash
	preview	relocate	unlike
		remodel	unnamed
			unselfish

#124

mis **words**	*pre* **words**	*re* **words**	*un* **words**
misbehave	precook	rebound	unaware
misfire	pregame	reconstruct	unbeaten
mishandle	prejudge	redirect	unbroken
mislead	premix	reenact	uncommon
misprint	preshrunk	refocus	uncooked
misspell		reform	undone
mistake		refresh	unfair
misuse		reorder	unhappy
		rephrase	

#125

mis **words**	*pre* **words**	*re* **words**	*un* **words**	OUT OF SORTS
misdeal	precut	recopy	unable	coolness
misgivings	prefix	recycle	unafraid	perfect
misguide	preheat	refinish	unbutton	sharpness
misinform	prepay	remind	unfold	spoonful
mislead	preset	research	unlock	
mistaken	presoak	reshape	unnoticed	
	pretest	rewrite		

Answer Keys:
Common Suffixes (#126-#131)

#126

er words	*est* words	*ful* words	*less* words
cleaner	boldest	cheerful	careless
colder	driest	harmful	endless
darker	oddest	helpful	friendless
firmer	quickest	hopeful	helpless
louder	roughest	lawful	meaningless
nearer	warmest	playful	painless
plainer		powerful	speechless
quieter		thoughtful	wordless

#127

er words	*est* words	*ful* words	*less* words
blacker	cheapest	armful	bottomless
harder	dearest	breathless	cloudless
nearer	fuller	colorful	helpless
rougher	loudest	doubtful	homeless
smaller	quietest	meaningful	jobless
sweeter		mouthful	limitless
		peaceful	priceless
		stressful	timeless
		tasteful	
		wishful	
		youthful	

#128

er words	*est* words	*ful* words	*less* words	OUT OF SORTS
brighter	cleanest	boastful	armless	mismatch
cleaner	clearest	graceful	endless	preview
darker	fairest	mouthful	faultless	recapture
stronger	firmest	playful	limitless	uncommon
sweeter	meanest	powerful	odorless	
		spoonful	painless	
		truthful	speechless	
		wasteful	thankless	

#129

ly words	*ness* words	*y* words
badly	awareness	chilly
cowardly	firmness	crispy
distinctly	moistness	dressy
eagerly	openness	greasy
gladly	ripeness	needy
lately	sharpness	rusty
legally	stiffness	sandy
likely	thinness	snowy
quietly	weakness	speedy
really		sugary
		tasty

#130

ly words	*ness* words	*y* words
busily	coolness	choppy
deadly	gladness	curly
directly	moistness	dressy
gloomily	readiness	noisy
greedily	ripeness	skinny
hastily	stillness	stormy
heavily	ugliness	windy
hungrily	vastness	worthy
lately	weariness	
loyally		
rudely		
safely		
strangely		

#131

ly words	*ness* words	*y* words	OUT OF SORTS
bravely	awareness	bumpy	react
costly	fondness	choppy	tasteless
crudely	fuzziness	dusty	unnoticed
daintily	goodness	filthy	wishful
deeply	happiness	foggy	
easily	haziness	gritty	
equally	scariness	rainy	
finally	weakness	thirsty	
legally			
shortly			

201

Answer Keys:

Final "K" Variations (#132–#134)

#132

c words	que words	ke words	k words	ck words
classic	brusque	evoke	artwork	bedrock
fabric	opaque	forsake	crosswalk	derrick
Pacific	plaque	keepsake	hallmark	gimmick
public	torque	mistake	homesick	oarlock
shellac	unique	provoke	network	stick
tonic		slowpoke	potluck	
zodiac		turnpike		

#133

c words	que words	ke words	k words	ck words
cosmic	antique	cupcake	bedrock	carsick
dynamic	boutique	earthquake	benchmark	cowlick
ethnic	clique	mistake	berserk	hammock
picnic	critique	namesake	cornstalk	
poetic	plaque	pancake	hallmark	
rustic		slowpoke	hassock	
tactic			landmark	
toxic				
tropic				

#134

c words	que words	ke words	k words	ck words	OUT OF SORTS
comic	baroque	clambake	cassock	fetlock	curtain
cubic	bisque	forsake	earmark	gimmick	keeping
dynamic	oblique	namesake	embark	haddock	kept
frantic	physique		homework	oarlock	kitchen
organic				paddock	
relic				ransack	
scenic				seasick	
tragic					

Answer Keys:

Consonant Alternations with Suffixes "ion" and "sion" (#135-#136)

#135

se, te—drop e and add ion

abbreviate – abbreviation
anticipate – anticipation
appreciate – appreciation
celebrate – celebration
complete – completion
create – creation
dictate – dictation
frustrate – frustration
fuse – fusion
hesitate – hesitation
incise – incision
invade – invasion
precise – precision
pretense – pretension
repulse – repulsion
revise – revision
supervise – supervision
tense – tension

de—drop de and add sion

allude – allusion
collide – collision
conclude – conclusion
corrode – corrosion
decide – decision
delude – delusion
evade – evasion
include – inclusion
persuade – persuasion
protrude – protrusion
provide – provision
seclude – seclusion

#136

se, te—drop e and add ion

circulate – circulation
confuse – confusion
decorate – decoration
evaporate – evaporation
fuse – fusion
hibernate – hibernation
illustrate – illustration
imitate – imitation
migrate – migration
navigate – navigation
operate – operation
pretense – pretension
revise – revision
televise – television
transfuse – transfusion
translate – translation

de—drop de and add sion

abrade – abrasion
collide – collision
conclude – conclusion
decide – decision
delude – delusion
deride – derision
divide – division
evade – evasion
explode – explosion
include – inclusion
intrude – intrusion
invade – invasion
provide – provision
seclude – seclusion

Answer Keys:

Adding the Suffixes "able" and "ible" to Base and Root Words (#137-#138)

#137

add able to base word

adapt
agree
approach
commend
credit
depend
detest
expand
favor
laugh
pay
prefer
question
reason
transfer

add ible to root word

aud
compat
cred
cruc
dirig
ed
gull
indel
invinc
irasc
leg
mand
ostens
tang
terr

#138

add able to base word

allow
commend
consider
detest
fashion
perish
predict
punish
read
reason
refill
remark
respect
season
transfer

add ible to root word

aud
compat
cred
cruc
ed
elig
feas
gull
incorrig
irasc
plaus
plaus
poss
tang
vis

Answer Keys:

Adding the Suffixes "able" and "ible" to Base and Root Words (#139–#140)

#139

drop the *e*	drop the *ate*	change the *y* to *i*
advise	appreciate	certify
assume	educate	deny
debate	estimate	envy
endure	imitate	identify
excite	irritate	justify
love	operate	modify
note	penetrate	pity
observe	separate	ply
pleasure	tolerate	rely
remove	vegetate	
size		

#140

drop the *e*	drop the *ate*	change the *y* to *i*
achieve	cultivate	classify
assume	debate	deny
breathe	irritate	envy
desire	negotiate	indentify
dispose	operate	modify
endure	venerate	ply
excite		quantify
excuse		rely
like		remedy
note		vary
observe		
oppose		
recycle		
reuse		

Answer Keys:

Doubling the Final Consonant in Multisyllablic Words (#141–#142)

#141

double the final consonant	don't double the final consonant
acquit	appear
admit	attend
allot	collect
begin	complain
confer	detour
control	detour
defer	exist
emit	explain
equip	insert
excel	prevent
forbid	repeat
forget	support
omit	
refer	
regret	
regret	
submit	
transfer	

#142

double the final consonant	don't double the final consonant
acquit	appear
admit	attend
allot	collect
commit	complain
confer	conduct
control	detour
defer	exist
equip	explain
expel	insert
forbid	patrol
forget	prevent
omit	repeat
permit	support
propel	
rebel	
refer	
regret	

Answer Keys:
Forming More Complex Plural Endings (#143-#144)

#143

change sis to ses	change a to ae	change us to i	change um to a
analysis	alga	alumnus	addendum
basis	antenna	cactus	bacterium
crisis	formula	cirrus	consortium
diagnosis	larva	focus	curriculum
oasis	nova	fungus	datum
synthesis	vertebra	nucleus	medium
		octopus	stratum
		radius	
		rhombus	
		stylus	
		syllabus	

#144

change ses	change a to ae	change us to i	change sis to um to a
analysis	alga	alumnus	addendum
basis	antenna	cactus	bacterium
crisis	formula	fungus	curriculum
nemesis	larva	nucleus	datum
oasis	nova	octopus	referendum
synopsis	persona	radius	solarium
thesis	vertebra	stimulus	stratum
		thesaurus	symposium

Answer Keys:
Common Prefixes: anti, auto, cat, circum (#145-#147)

#145

anti	auto	cat, cata	circum
anticlimactic	autobiography	cataclysm	circumference
antidote	autocrat	catacomb	circumfuse
antifreeze	autograph	catalogue	circumpolar
antihistamine	automatic	catapult	circumspect
antipathy	automaton	cataract	circumstance
antiseptic	automobile	catastrophe	circumvent
antitoxin	autonomy	catatonic	
antitrust	autopsy		
antiwar			

#146

anti	auto	cat, cata	circum
anticlimactic	autobiography	cataclysm	circumference
antifreeze	autocrat	catacomb	circumfuse
antihistamine	autograph	catalepsy	circumnavigate
antipathy	automatic	catalogue	circumpolar
antipathy	automaton	catapult	circumspect
antiseptic	automobile	cataract	circumstance
antitrust	autonomy	catastrophe	circumvent
antiwar	autopsy		

#147

anti	auto	cat, cata	circum	OUT OF SORTS
antibiotic	autobiography	cataclysm	circumference	decade
anticlimactic	autocrat	catacomb	circumfuse	malfunction
antifreeze	automatic	catalogue	circumpolar	postpone
antihistamine	automaton	catapult	circumspect	transplant
antisocial	automobile	cataract	circumstance	
antitrust	autonomy	catastrophe	circumvent	
antiwar	autopsy			

Answer Keys:

Common Prefixes: inter, intra, mal, peri (#148–#150)

#148

inter	intra	mal	peri
interact	intramural	maladjusted	pericardium
intercede	intrastate	malady	peridontal
interchange	intravenous	malaria	perigee
interface		malefactor	perimeter
interject		malevolent	period
interlace		malfunction	periphery
interlock		malign	periscope
interloper		malinger	
intermission		malnutrition	
interrupt		malpractice	

#149

inter	intra	mal	peri
interact	intramural	maladjusted	pericardium
intercede	intrastate	malady	peridontal
interchange	intravenous	malaria	perigee
intercollegiate		malcontent	perimeter
interface		malefactor	period
interlock		malfeasance	peripatetic
interloper		malfunction	periphery
intermediary		malign	periscope
intermission		malnutrition	
		malpractice	

#150

inter	intra	mal	peri	OUT OF SORTS
interact	intramural	maladjusted	pericardium	autocrat
intercede	intrastate	malady	peridontal	catapult
interchange	intravenous	malaria	perigee	circumvent
interlock		malcontent	perimeter	translate
interloper		malefactor	period	
intermediary		malfunction	peripatetic	
intermission		malign	periscope	
interpret		malpractice		

Answer Keys:

Common Prefixes: post, pro, super, trans (#151–#153)

#151

post	pro	super	trans
postdate	proceed	superficial	transfuse
postdoctoral	proclaim	superman	transit
posterior	profane	supermarket	translate
posterity	profess	supernatural	transplant
postmeridian	proficient	superpower	transport
postpone	program	supersede	transpose
postscript	progress	supersonic	
	pronounce	supervision	
	provide		

#152

post	pro	super	trans
posterior	proceed	supercilious	transatlantic
posterity	proclaim	superman	transcend
posthumous	prodigy	supermarket	transcribe
postpone	profile	supersede	transfigure
postscript	profound	supersonic	transgress
	progress	superstition	transit
	prohibit	supervision	transmit
	propel		transparent
	provide		transpose

#153

post	pro	super	trans	OUT OF SORTS
postdate	proceed	superficial	transatlantic	antitrust
posterior	proclaim	superimpose	transfer	autograph
posterity	prohibit	superman	transgress	malaria
posthumous	promote	supersede	transpire	prophet
postpone	propel	supersonic	transplant	
postscript	proportion	superstition	transport	
		supervision	transpose	

Answer Keys:

Number-Related Prefixes (#154-#159)

#154

bi	cent	dec	mon, mono	multi	oct, octa
biennial	centennial	decade	monarchy	multicolored	octagon
bilateral	centigrade	decameter	monolith	multifaceted	octave
bilingual	centimeter	December	monorail	multiple	octillion
bimonthly	centipede	decimal	monotheism	multitude	October
biped	century	decimeter	monotone		
biweekly			monotonous		

#155

bi	cent	dec	mon, mono	multi	oct, octa
bipartisan	centigrade	decade	monarchy	multifamily	octagon
biped	centimeter	decagon	monastery	multiple	octahedron
bipolar	centipede	decameter	monograph	multiplex	octave
bisect	century	December	monologue	multiply	octet
bivalve	percent		monopoly	multitude	octopus
			monorail		

#156

bi	cent	dec	mon, mono	multi	oct, octa	OUT OF SORTS
biennial	centenarian	decade	monograph	multilateral	octagon	monastery
bimonthly	centigrade	decagon	monolith	multiple	octahedron	mountain
biped	centipede	decameter	monologue	multiplex	octet	postpone
bipolar	century	December	monotone	multitude	October	supersonic
biweekly					octopus	

#157

pent	poly	quad	semi	tri	uni
pentagon	polychrome	quadrangle	semiannual	triad	unicorn
pentameter	polygon	quadrant	semicircle	triangle	unicycle
pentathlon	polyphonic	quadriceps	semicolon	triceps	uniform
pentatonic	polysyllabic	quadrille	semitropical	trio	unity
	polytechnic	quadruplets	semiyearly	triplet	universal
				tripod	

#158

pent	poly	quad	semi	tri	uni
pentadactyl	polygon	quadrant	semicircle	tricycle	unicycle
pentagon	polygraph	quadrille	semicolon	triennial	unilateral
pentameter	polynomial	quadruped	semidetached	trinity	unique
pentathlon	polyphony	quadruple	semifinal	triplet	unison
Pentecost			semisolid		unit
			semiyearly		unity
					university

#159

pent	poly	quad	semi	tri	uni	OUT OF SORTS
pentagon	polyhedron	quadriceps	semicircle	tricolor	unilateral	autograph
pentameter	polynominal	quadrille	semicolon	trio	unison	bisect
pentathlon	polyphony	quadruped	semiprivate	triplet	unite	prophet
pentatonic	polysyllabic	quadruplets	semisolid	tripod	universal	transport
			semiweekly		universe	

Answer Keys:

Common Greek Root Words (#160-#163)

#160

aer	arch	aster, astr	bio	centr	cris, crit
aerate	anarchy	asterisk	antibiotic	centrifugal	crisis
aerie	archangel	asteroid	biography	centrist	criterion
aerobatics	archduke	astrology	biology	concentric	critic
aerobic	archetype	astronaut	biopsy	eccentric	criticize
aerosol	architect	astrophysics	symbiotic	egocentric	critique

#161

chron	cycl	dem	derm	geo	gram
chronic	cyclist	democracy	epidermis	geocentric	anagram
chronicle	cyclone	democratic	hypodermic	geode	grammar
chronology	motorcycle	demographic	pachyderm	geographic	hologram
chronometer	recycle	endemic	taxidermy	geology	program
synchronize	tricycle	epidemic		geophysics	telegram
				geothermal	

#162

graph	hydr	log	meter	micro	phon
autograph	hydra	analogy	barometer	microbe	headphone
graphite	hydrant	apologize	diameter	microchip	phonics
photograph	hydrate	dialogue	kilometer	microcosm	saxophone
polygraph	hydraulic	ecology	millimeter	micrometer	symphony
seismograph	hydroplane	logical	speedometer		telephone
telegraph					

#163

photo	phys	pol, polis	scope	sphere	tele
photocell	astrophysics	Annapolis	gyroscope	bathysphere	telecast
photocopier	geophysics	megalopolis	horoscope	biosphere	telegram
photogenic	metaphysics	metropolis	microscope	hemisphere	telegraph
photography	physical	police	periscope	stratosphere	telepathy
photometry	physique	policy	stethoscope		telethon
		politician			

Answer Keys:

Common Latin Root Words (#164-#165)

#164

aud	bene, beni	cap	ced, ceas	cide	clud, clos
audio	benefactor	capillary	antecedent	concise	closet
audit	beneficial	capital	cease	excise	disclose
audition	beneficiary	capitalize	intercede	germicide	foreclose
auditorium	benefit	capitol	recede	incise	preclude
auditory	benign	captain	secede	pesticide	seclude

#165

cor, corp	cred	dic, dict	duce, duct	equa, equi	fac, fact, fect
corporal	accredit	dedicate	abduct	equable	defect
corporation	credence	diction	conductor	equation	facsimile
corpse	credentials	dictionary	deduction	equilibrium	faction
corpulent	credible	predicate	educate	equity	factory
	credit	prediction	induct	equivalent	manufacture
	discredit				

Answer Keys:
Common Latin Root Words (#166-#170)

#166

fer	form	grac, grat	grad, gress	hab, hib	ject
conference	deform	congratulate	centigrade	habit	conjecture
differ	formal	grace	congress	habitat	dejected
ferry	formation	gracious	degradable	habituate	objection
infer	formula	grateful	regressing	inhabit	projectile
inference	information	gratify	transgress	inhibit	
		gratuity			

#167

lit	loc, loq	man	mem	miss, mit	mob, mot
illiterate	colloquial	manacle	memento	commission	immobile
literacy	elocution	manage	memoir	emissary	locomotion
literal	eloquent	maneuver	memorable	missile	mobile
literary	ventriloquist	manicure	memorial	missionary	motivate
literature		manual	memory	permission	promote

#168

numer	ped	pens, pend	port	pos, pone	prim,princ
innumerable	centipede	appendix	deportment	impostor	pimary
number	expedite	compensate	export	opposite	primate
numerator	millipede	dispense	important	position	prince
numerous	pedestrian	impending	portable	preposition	principal
		pendant	portfolio	transpose	
		pendulum	report		
			transport		

#169

quer, ques	scrib, script	sent, sens	sist, stat	spec, spect	tain
acquire	description	consensus	consistent	auspicious	abstain
inquisition	inscribe	consent	desist	circumspect	entertain
query	postscript	dissent	insistent	inspector	maintain
question	prescription	sensation	station	specimen	pertain
request	scribble	sentry		spectator	
require	scripture				

#170

tract	val	ven, vent	vers, vert	vid, vis	voc, vok
attract	devaluate	convention	advertise	evident	avocation
extraction	evaluate	eventual	conversation	invisible	evoke
protract	valiant	intervene	convert	providence	provoke
traction	validate	prevent	introvert	supervision	vocabulary
			inverse	televise	vocation
			reverse		
			traverse		
			universe		

Does your school or school district need a WORD STUDY program?

Author Sheron Brown is available to teach workshops on both word sorting and multi-syllabic word study activities.

The All Sorts of Sorts Workshop

Word study should be an integral part of every classroom's language arts block, whether primary or upper grade. Word sorting is a particularly unique word study activity that enables students to focus on word patterns, word parts, spelling rules and generalizations, and word meanings through a "compare and contrast" activity. Once students have been taught the five types of word sort procedures they can independently focus on their own word development stage while performing the various word sorting activities.

Highlights
In this workshop you will learn:
- a quick and easy assessment procedure to determine each student's word study developmental level.
- how to group your students for effective word study instruction in a twenty-minute daily format.
- the five kinds of word sorts, the benefits of each type of sort, and how to teach your students to do them.
- how to organize your classroom for additional word study activities such as word hunts, and word study notebooks.
- how to monitor each student's word study progress and how to determine each student's "next steps" for word study activities.

Multi-syllabic Words Workshop

As students progress through the upper elementary and middle school grades, word study focuses on multi-syllabic words containing many common prefixes, suffixes, vowels and vowel combinations. Using the approach of directly teaching these common prefixes, suffixes, vowels, and vowel combinations, students can actively decode and attach meaning to the many multi-syllabic words they encounter in content area and reading texts. Additional study of the most common Greek and Latin root words also aids the students in making meaning from words.

Highlights
In this workshop you will learn:
- the most frequently encountered prefixes, suffixes, vowels and vowel combinations and how to present them to your students in a direct instruction format.
- a quick "circle front, circle back and underline" word attack procedure to teach your students to help them actively decode any multi-syllabic words they encounter.
- a quick and easy instructional format to present the common Greek and Latin root words along with their meanings.
- specific activities and suggestions for classroom management and multi-syllabic word study for vocabulary building.

To find out more about these exciting workshops
call 650-598-0400 or e-mail annlinehan@earthlink.net